Arklow Shipping

A Group Fleet History
by
W J Harvey

The **Arklow Valour** seen discharging animal feed at the West Twin Silo, Belfast, clearly displays her box type hold – ideal for the bulk cargo trades in which the company specialises.

(Alan Geddes)

Front cover : The **Arklow Spray**, moored at Manisty Wharf on the Manchester Ship Canal, is passed by the **Arklow River** which is on her way to Manchester.

(Arend Groen)

Contents

By the same author: -

SHAMROCK SHIPPING – Including the David Dorman Group   (World Ship Society Ltd., Windsor, 2004; ISBN 0 9543310-3-6)
The history of two Irish-based companies from 1888 and 1881 respectively, through unification to today's much diminished shipping activity.

SAFMARINE - The South African Marine Corporation Ltd – A Group History
   (World Ship Society, Gravesend, 2002; ISBN 0 905617-98-3)
The history of the Cape Town based company from 1946 until its 1999 break up and sale. In association with C. R. Mackenzie.

THE CLYDE SHIPPING COMPANY   (P. J. Telford, Canterbury, 2002; ISBN 0 9542527-0-5)
The history of the Glasgow based Company from 1815 until its 2000 acquisition by Cory Towage Ltd. In association with P. J. Telford.

CORY TOWAGE LTD – A Group History   (World Ship Society, Gravesend, 2000; ISBN 0 905617-93-2)
The history of the company and its owned, managed, and chartered vessels, together with the fleets of its subsidiary and associated companies.

SHIPS IN FOCUS – BLUE FUNNEL LINE   (Ships in Focus Publications, Longton, 1998; ISBN 1 901703-00-2)
A pictorial fleet history of the Liverpool-based shipping group. In association with John Clarkson and Roy Fenton.

HADLEY   (The World Ship Society, Gravesend, 1997; ISBN 0 905617-83-5)
The history of the Hadley Shipping Company Ltd., and its associate companies.

HEAD LINE (G. Heyn & Sons Ltd.)   (The World Ship Society, Kendal, 1990; ISBN 0 905617-53-3)
The history of the Ulster Steamship Company Ltd., and its associate companies.

STENA (1939 – 1989)   (Stena Ab, Gothenburg, 1990; ISBN 91 85786-411)
The first fifty years of the Swedish-controlled multinational shipping and trading group.)

EMPIRE TUGS   (World Ship Society, Kendal, 1988; ISBN 0 905617-47-9)
The history of the EMPIRE-prefixed, British Government tugs, introduced during WW 2. In association with Ken Turrell.

Published in the United Kingdom by Bernard McCall, 400 Nore Road, Portishead, Bristol BS20 8EZ, U.K.
Telephone/fax : 01275 846178. E-mail : bernard@coastalshipping.co.uk. Website : www.coastalshipping.co.uk
Printed in the United Kingdom by The Amadeus Press, Cleckheaton, West Yorkshire, BD19 4TQ.
Telephone : 01274 863210; fax : 01274 863211. E-mail : info@amadeuspress.co.uk
All distribution enquiries should be addressed to the publisher.
© 2004   W. J. Harvey and Bernard McCall.

ISBN 1 – 902953 - 15 - 0

Introduction.

Arklow, 65 kilometres south of Dublin on the east coast of the Republic of Ireland, has for many years boasted a seafaring tradition of many facets.

Many local families have spawned thriving maritime businesses through the passage of time, none more so, in recent years, than the Tyrrell and Hall families. They have come to the fore and seen their endeavours flourish since the formation of Arklow Shipping in 1966. Although the career of the company is relatively short, nearing 40 years, it is steeped in family maritime traditions.

The purpose of this work is not to analyse the business workings of the Group but to concentrate on the tools of its trade, and record the development of the fleet as it has grown from strength to strength.

Arklow: A Brief Historical Overview

Arklow, a small port on the east coast of the Republic of Ireland, is home to the Tyrrell family, one that has been associated with the sea for as far back as one would like to trace.

The people of Arklow have also had a long association, primarily in the fishing trades. Between seasons the smack owners carried small quantities of cargo to supplement their earnings. About 300 years ago copper mines were established at Avoca, about six miles upstream, and these enticed the boat owners to become part-time traders in a small way at first, but by the early nineteenth century, the mines were having a dramatic effect on the prosperity of the port of Arklow.

In the 1830s the King of Naples, who also ruled Sicily, imposed a restrictive tax on the export of sulphur ore from Sicily. This commodity was in much demand by factories of England, and as a result, supplies were sought elsewhere. One of the main by-products of the Avoca mines was sulphur and because of the proximity of the source this attracted a rapid increase in demand.

Harvest King of 1879, a schooner built at Runcorn.

(Author's collection)

However, the supply was not easily obtained due to the erratic flow of the river combined with the poor infrastructure of the port. At this time the boats were hauled up on the beach and only pushed into the water as required.

The merchants of the town recognised the potential of a good port and made an approach to the local seafarers with the view to forming a ship-owning partnership under the traditional 1/64th share system. Agreement having been reached, business flourished and toward the end of the nineteenth century some 80 trading vessels and 150 fishing vessels were based at the port.

For the next seventy or so years the port continued to boom but there was the First World War looming and when it arrived the Arklow fleets were reduced to a position that was to have an irreversible effect on the fortunes of the port. Following hostilities the steamship and subsequently the motorship were to sweep aside the remnants of the sailing fleets. Arklow owners were not sentimentally involved with sail but stuck with it for financial reasons. As a result they had to compromise to survive and this saw many vessels having auxiliary engines fitted. When this was actioned a corresponding amount of sail was removed, mainly on topsail. The Halls and Tyrrells were two of the more prominent families operating these vessels from Arklow. The Kearon family was another.

Industry of 1848.

(Author's collection)

Happy Harry of 1894 showing evidence of auxiliary power.

(Author's collection)

Mary B Mitchell of 1892 seen during the Second World War shortly before her loss in December 1944.

(Author's collection)

Tyrronall *before her rebuild.*

Invermore *(left) and* **James Postlethwaite** *leaving Cork in 1947. Both were schooners. The* **Invermore** *was built by J.Tyrrell and Sons, Arklow, and owned by Mrs E.Tyrrell, of Arklow. The* **James Postlethwaite,** *built in 1881 by W.Ashburner, of Barrow, was sold to E.K.Hall, Arklow, in 1928.*

The derelict remains of **Invermore**, a vessel that gave its name to one of the numerous companies in the Arklow Shipping Group.

(Author's collection)

Having weathered this problem, the next were looming over the horizon. Firstly there was the division of Ireland into the states of Northern Ireland and Irish Republic or Free State. Secondly there was the Depression which resulted in many of the vessels being taken to quiet inlets along the river and placed in lay-up. Those vessels that were not left to rot had their machinery uprated but despite this owners were still fighting a losing battle. Soon another war had arrived, as had all the accompanying problems that were to have adverse effects on the port and associated trade. After the Second World War the inevitable happened when the first motor powered cargo vessel was purchased by the Tyrrell family. This vessel was a War Prize and when delivered she was renamed **Tyrronall**. Although this name ends in ALL, most subsequent vessels owned by James Tyrrell carried names ending in ELL. The reason was simple. It was three letters from each of her three participant owners names – **Tyr**rell; Kea**ron**; H**all**.

During the years following the Second World War, the remaining auxiliary sailing vessels were replaced with more modern tonnage placing the Port of Arklow firmly into a new era in its history. The fact that the motor vessel had arrived was not alone to be the saviour of the port. The Tyrrell family was to give serious support to the development of the port and was joined in the early 1960s by the Hall family. Both were amongst several well-known Arklow families operating fleets of vessels under their own banners.

Arklow Shipping: The Birth of an Enterprise

Arklow River, newly purchased, at Dublin on 8 May 1984, still in Fisher colours, showing her Dublin registry.

(Author's collection / T. O'Connalain)

The independent method of operation by these families was such that a vessel owned by Tyrrell could discharge in Dublin and sail in ballast to Liverpool to load, whilst a Hall-owned vessel could well have discharged at Liverpool and sailed to Dublin to load, in both cases uneconomically.

So it came about that, in 1966, after due consideration and forward planning, the Tyrrell family decided there was a necessity for an umbrella management-type organisation to co-ordinate the operations of all the local fleets. The intention was that all the operators would pool their resources as a method of reducing operating costs and overheads.

Tyrrells then issued an open invitation to all Arklow-based owners to join in the proposed co-operative. The only positive response came from the Hall family and so Arklow Shipping was founded to control the combined fleet of eight vessels. Kearon, the other principal Arklow family, opted to remain independent and as predicted was subsequently to withdraw from the business.

Although founded as a co-operative in 1966 the name of Arklow Shipping Ltd. was not to appear as a registered shipowner until 1970 when it purchased a ship in its own right. This small Dutch-built coaster was, appropriately, renamed **Arklow**.

James Tyrrell was one of, if not THE, main shareholder since the outset but confusion was to set in over the next few years as various other directors within the company were to incorporate their own new companies such as Bay Shipping Ltd., (1971), and Vale Shipping Ltd., (1972), with their vessels also carrying the ARKLOW prefix. Each company initially wholly owned its ship(s) without cross shareholdings but all were operated under Arklow Shipping Ltd. management.

Following the death of Guernsey shipowner Peter Dorey in the Fastnet Race, his wife continued to run the Guernsey-based shipping business successfully for several years but after problems with manning etc, decided to offer the company for sale as a going concern.

During 1982/83 Arklow Shipping entered into protracted negotiations with the Dorey family's legal representatives regarding a potential purchase of the business, although not necessarily the vessels. Those talks, however, failed to reach agreement. The end result saw Dorey's business pass to Fishers of Barrow.

Although Arklow had, over the years, boasted a considerable fleet of vessels, the owners were somewhat annoyed that those vessels had to be registered at Dublin. This was mainly because of the absence of a Customs House at the small port of Arklow. However, with the demise of the State-owned Irish Shipping Ltd. in the 1980s, Arklow Shipping Ltd., found itself as the proud operator of what had become the largest single fleet of merchant vessels under the Irish flag, and as such, made representations to the authorities to have Arklow declared a port of registry.

Following lengthy deliberations by the authorities, the "request" was granted and from 1988 the fleet was transferred from Dublin to Arklow registry, a fitting tribute to the strivings of the Tyrrell family, amongst others, to develop the port and the Irish merchant fleet.

Around this time investment was being placed for newly-built tonnage as opposed to previous policy of purchasing mostly second-hand vessels. Having studied the market trends, the partners began to construct vessels of the "low-air-draught" design. These vessels were designed to maximise hull size with little or no superstructure. The wheelhouse was mounted on a hydraulic ram enabling it to be raised for sea journeys and lowered for passing under low bridges enabling the vessel to voyage far inland to such places as those ports on the rivers Rhine and Ruhr, in Germany. This negated the requirement for cargo destined for inland locations to be trans-shipped into what could have been several barges at the coastal ports for onward passage because the traditional coaster could not negotiate the numerous low inland bridges.

Arklow Bay at anchor off Gravesend, showing her hydraulic bridge in the lowered position.

(Author's collection / D. Hocquard)

Inisheer was one of several larger multi-purpose vessels acquired. Here we see her outward bound in the River Mersey with a cargo of containers on 26 July 1989. At the time, she traded between Ellesmere Port and Belfast or Warrenpoint.

(Iain McCall)

Henceforth the group never looked back, going from strength to strength, building a fleet of modern state-of-the-art vessels as replacements for the obsolescent second-hand tonnage on which it had built its foundations.The company was always looking for markets in which to gain experience and to expand. Those experiments saw numerous types of vessels acquired over the years. They ranged from small, traditional coastal vessels, through mini bulk carriers, a tug and a large cement carrier to multi-purpose container carriers. As progress was made, vessels grew in size in parallel, either through acquisition or surgery being carried out on existing vessels. There were a few upsets along the way, however, when the almost-new **Arklow Victor** capsized and sank and **Arklow Castle** (1) was wrecked on the French coast.

Another expansion programme was initiated when a series of "S" class vessels was ordered from Dutch shipbuilders in 1994. These ice-strengthened vessels were also capable of limited container transportation, as were the "M" and "V" classes before.

Good experience operating a vessel the size of **Arklow Beach**, prompted the placing of an order for two larger vessels of almost 5,000 gross tons with Appledore Shipbuilders. This latter pair was to be quite versatile in that they were strengthened for heavy cargoes and their bottoms strengthened to enable loading or unloading whilst aground. Additionally they were strengthened for ice navigation and for being unloaded with grabs up to 10 tons in weight, making them very suitable for the bulk cargo market.

Arklow Bridge inward bound on the Manchester Ship Canal passes an unidentified member of the Arklow fleet at Runcorn Salt Works.

(Neil Burns)

James Tyrrell

Sheila Tyrrell

Barry Tyrrell

Three family members who are the driving force behind the company.

(Author's collection)

Opportunities arose for the purchase of further quality second-hand tonnage at the end of 1996 and 1997 when six vessels were acquired, two by the associated Coastal Shipping PLC.

In 1998 it was decided that due to lack of Irish Government support in the form of tax incentives for shipowners, several of the Arklow fleet would become "flagged out". Initially two new vessels under construction in Netherlands were registered at Zaandam in that country to take advantage of Dutch tax incentives for shipowners.

It was announced during 1999 that Arklow Shipping Ltd., was to expand into the Netherlands with the acquisition of Heinrich Hanno & Company B.V. That acquisition was initially renamed Hanno Shipping B.V. and was to remain a Dutch flag operation along with their newly constructed vessels. It was during 2002 restyled as Arklow Shipping Nederland B. V.

Having continued to successfully market the Appledore twins, the company took a bold step when the opportunity presented itself. A pair of multi-purpose self-discharging bulk carriers, originally operated by the Norwegian Jebsen Group, became available at separate auctions, months apart. The company successfully tendered for the pair, both in need of a good overhaul. These acquisitions brought another increase in size, and also revived two old "D" names. The first was named **Arklow Dawn**, as a dawn of a new era, followed by **Arklow Day**. Successful marketing and securing of forward contracts saw a third similar sized vessel added as **Arklow Dusk**.

The **Arklow Dusk** was the third member of the D class.

(Author's collection)

A class of five "R" vessels was ordered from a Dutch shipbuilding group for 2002/03 delivery as replacements for the older "M" and "V" classes that were being disposed of. As with the "S" class they were of the more traditional design unlike their predecessors of the elevating bridge type. This influx of new tonnage brought with it a major restructuring of fleet ownership.

Replacement and expansion continued unabated. A decision was taken in 2002 to replace the ageing "D" vessels. Two large "W" class bulk carriers were ordered in Japan together with the option for a third, whilst a second tranche of five "R" class vessels was ordered from Dutch builders in 2003, for delivery over an 18-month period. During mid-2004 rumours began to circulate among the shipping fraternity that further changes were being planned. The "M", "V" and "F" classes were to be disposed of in favour of a new class of vessel that could number as many as 12 units, and so the story of a proactively managed company rolls on.

The **Arklow Moor** was photographed in the Solent on 24 April 1997.

(Chris Bancroft)

A Hanno Portfolio

The **Scotia** is at No. 4 Quay in Kings Dock, Swansea, on 15 May 1998 and is about to start loading a cargo of coal duff for Rotterdam.

(Bill Moore)

Tilbury Dock is the setting for the **Cemile** on 13 July 2002.

(Ian Willett)

Two photographs to please the many readers who like to see ships in a landscape. The **Magdalena** discharges rock salt from Kilroot at Giants Wharf, Briton Ferry, on 24 March 2000.

(Bill Moore)

Bristol's City Docks see only about one cargo ship each year, calling to load heavy or awkward cargoes manufactured by an engineering company adjacent to the Cumberland Basin. On 22 November 2001, the **Ikiena** arrived from Drogheda and loaded silos for delivery to the River Tees. She was photographed in the lock as she departed. The fashionable area of Clifton dominates the background and a section of Brunel's famous suspension bridge is visible to the left.

(Cedric Catt)

*The **Shevrell** (3) awaits her turn to load china clay at Fowey on what is evidently a busy day in May 1987.*

(Stan Tedford)

Acknowledgements

During the course of my research into this rather complex company, many people have rendered assistance over the years. To them I now offer my sincere thanks.

Darlow, William - (now deceased), for letting me browse his records of Irish shipping companies.

Hackman, Rowan - (now deceased), for delving into his shipbuilding records for obscure dates. Unfortunately he was unable to conclude that activity.

Lloyd's Register of Shipping, Information Section, Fenchurch St., London
  Barbara Jones, Anne Cowne and Emma Haxhaj, for the use of the relevant *Lloyd's Registers* and other publications held by the library.

Maritime Information Publishing Group – (now part of Lloyd's Register Fairplay at Redhill).

Leslie Spurling, **Peter Brazier**, **Chris Cheetham** and **Richard Pride** - for referring to their records to confirm, or otherwise, my own research, under the usual confidentiality constraints, and for pointing me in the direction of subsequent sources.

Mayes, Gil - for his good offices in validating and supplementing data from his extensive database.

O' Conallain, Terry - for his advice and knowledge on particular Irish shipping matters, and for his presence behind a camera.

Sweeney, Pat - for his advice and knowledge on particular Irish shipping matters.

The Amadeus Press - for bringing the book to a successful conclusion.

If anyone has been overlooked then please also accept my thanks, as this was not deliberate.

Photographs

These are credited to the known source below each photograph. The author recently acquired a large quantity of photographs of company vessels from a private collector. Unfortunately, not all of those within that collection have an identifiable source on the rear. My apologies therefore are offered to anyone recognising a photograph that has been incorrectly credited.

Notes On The Ship Histories

The small number above the name on later vessels is the International Maritime Organisation (IMO) Identity No. That remains with a vessel for life and must now be displayed prominently on the vessel exterior. Examples seen so far have usually been on the stern near the name.

The first line contains the fleet chronology number, ship name, the number of vessels that have carried the name in the fleet, (in brackets) and the period in the fleet (in brackets).

The second line contains the O. N. = Official Number, (where known); g. = gross, n. = net, and d. = deadweight tonnages, followed by the dimensions between perpendiculars for earlier vessels given in feet and tenths of feet. From 1956 overall dimensions were given in feet and inches. Lloyd's Register changed to metric dimensions overall in 1975.

The third line contains the number of engines (if more than one), followed by the number of cylinders followed by the number of S. C. = stroke cycle and S. A. = single acting. (e.g. 4 S.C.S.A.). This is succeeded by (cylinder sizes x stroke length) then by machinery type, (where known) and the manufacturer thereof, followed by the NHP. = nominal horse power, (e.g. 115 nhp on early vessels) or BHP. = brake horse power, (e.g. 2,500 bhp). That is then followed by the vessel speed (where known) and any supplementary propulsion units (on later vessels). The final section contains the ship history commencing with any specific description of the vessel, keel laying, launch or completion dates (whichever are known), the shipbuilder, (Yard No.) etc., followed by the vessel's career.

The Fleets

Captain R. V. T. Hall.

Arklow

Operated under the auspices HALL & TYRRELL LTD. following a 1966 merger with MICHAEL G. TYRRELL. q.v.

H.1. **Kilbride**   (1966 - 1971)
O.N. 166692.   321g.   143n.   325d.   131.5' x 24.6' x 8.8'.
6-cyl. 2 S.C.S.A. (265mm x 345mm) oil engine by Crossley Bros. Ltd., Manchester. 116nhp. / 330 bhp. 9 kts.

11.7.1942 : Launched as **Empire Reynard** by Richards Iron Works Ltd., Lowestoft, (Yard No. 301), for The Ministry of War Shipping, London. 10.1942 : Completed. 1943 : Transferred to the Royal Netherlands Government, (Nederland Trading & Shipping Committee Ltd., London), and renamed **Westerhaven**. 1946 : Sold to Société Anomino Jean Negri, France, and renamed **Orsuro**. 1949 : Sold to Compagnie Charentaise de Transports Remorquages et Sauvetages, France, and renamed **Chassiron**. 1951 : Sold to R. V. T. Hall, Dublin, and renamed **Kilbride**. 1966 : As a result of a merger, operators restyled Hall & Tyrrell Ltd., although vessel remained registered under R. V. T. Hall. 12.1971 : Sold to T. R. Rive, Hitchen, Herts, retaining Dublin registry. (It was intended that the vessel would be renamed **Peacock Venture** and be operated by Peacock Shipping Ltd., Guernsey). 1973 : Sold to Mrs. Joyce Hercock, Sheffield, to have been renamed **Joyce**, registered at Hull, but resold for demolition to Albert Draper & Son Ltd., Hull, who completed work during 11.1973.

In a scene simply oozing atmosphere, **Kilbride** is seen at Dublin in June 1965.

(Stan Tedford)

H.2. **River Avoca** (1)   (1966 - 1976)
O.N. 400330.   384g.   137n.   447d.   143.9' x 24.7' x 7.9'.
As built : 4-cyl. 2 S.C.S.A. (250mm x 420mm) oil engine by British Polar Engines Ltd., Glasgow. 350 bhp. 9 kts.
Post 1971 : 6-cyl. 4 S.C.S.A. (625mm x 800mm) vee type oil engine by the Caterpillar Tractor Company, Peoria, Illinois. 425 bhp.

20.7.1947 : Launched as **Stevonia** by Goole Shipbuilding & Repairing Company Ltd., Goole, (Yard No. 467), for J. Wharton & Sons, Keadby, subsequently J. Wharton (Shipping) Ltd. 2.1948 : Completed. 1962 : Sold to R. V. T. Hall, Dublin. 1963 : Renamed **River Avoca**. 1966 : As a result of a merger, operators restyled Hall & Tyrrell Ltd., although vessel remained registered under R. V. T. Hall. 12.1971 : Re-engined. 1976 : Sold to Allyx Maritime Enterprises Inc., Panama, and renamed **River Karoon**. 1981 : Demolished.

Again there is plenty of historical interest in this view of the **River Avoca** loading scrap in Belfast in November 1970.

(Stan Tedford)

Captain Michael G. Tyrrell
Arklow

Operated under the auspices of HALL & TYRRELL LTD. following a merger with Captain R. V. T. HALL. q.v.

MG.1. *Avondale* (1966 - 1974)
O.N. 400214. 303g. 143n. 374d. 144' 5" x 23' 8" x 9' 1"
4-cyl. 4 S.C.S.A. (280mm x 400mm) oil engine by Motorenfabriek "De Industrie", Alphen a/d IJssel. 195 bhp. 8 kts.

29.6.1950 : Launched as *Navis* by Scheepswerke A. Apol, Wirdum, (Yard No.164), for Gebrouders van Diepen, Groningen, (Kamp's Scheepsvaart en Handelmaatschappij N.V., managers), Netherlands. 9.1950 : Completed. 1953 : Sold to W. J. Kramer, Groningen, (same manager). 1956 : Renamed *Aegir*. 1958 : Sold to Michael G. Tyrrell, Dublin, and renamed *Avondale*. 1966 : As a result of a merger, operators restyled Hall & Tyrrell Ltd., although vessel remained registered under M. G. Tyrrell. 1974 : Sold to Inter Island Shipping Ltd., Bangor, N. Ireland, and renamed *Orlock*. 1976 : Sold to R. W. C. Gillis and F. J. Lewis, Newquay and Torquay respectively, trading as Gillew Shipping Company Ltd., Newquay, and renamed *Commerce*; registered at London. 1977 : R. W. C. Gillew became sole proprietor. 1978 : Sold to Galaxy Shoppe (Anguilla) Ltd., London. 1989 : Reported as having been scuttled.

*Once again Belfast is the setting as the **Avondale** makes her way through the port in February 1972.*

(Stan Tedford)

The following vessel was owned by M. G. Tyrrell after the formation of Arklow Shipping Ltd. It was not however declared as part of the Arklow consortium.

MG.2. *Joan T* (1973 - 1985)
O.N. 401216. 397g. 172n. 550d. 152' 7" x 25' 6" x 11' 2½"
8-cyl. 4 S.C.S.A. (235mm x 330mm) oil engine by Maschinenbau Augsburg - Nürnberg (MAN), Augsburg. 410 bhp. 10 kts

18.12.1958 : Launched as *Scheldt* by Scheepsbouw Gebrouders Barkmeijer, Veirverlaten, (Yard No. 154), for Wm. H. Muller & Company (Batavier) Ltd., London. 2.4.1959 : Completed. 1969 : Owners restyled as Wm. H. Muller & Company (London) Ltd. 1970 : Sold to Metcalf Motor Coasters Ltd., London, and renamed *Thomas M*. 1973 : Purchased by Michael G. Tyrrell, Arklow, and renamed *Joan T*. 1985 : Sold to M. & H. Shipping Ltd., (Ireland-based owners), Douglas, Isle of Man. 1986 : Renamed *Elfi*. 1987 : Sold to Windlass Marine Ltd., Douglas, Isle of Man. 3.1987 : Foundered.

Joan T *heads up the River Mersey and approaches the Manchester Ship Canal at Eastham, probably bound for Runcorn to load a cargo of salt.*

(Bernard McCall)

James Tyrrell Ltd.
Arklow

T.1. **Alfred Mason** (1966 - 1968)
O.N. 137097. 305g. 144n. 365d. 127.0' x 23.6' x 10.4'.
As built : 4-cyl. 2 S.C.S.A. ($16\frac{1}{2}$" x $18\frac{1}{10}$") oil engine by J. och C. G. Bolinders Mekaniska Verksted, Stockholm. 91 nhp.
Post 1922 : 4-cyl. 2 S.C.S.A. ($16\frac{1}{2}$" x $18\frac{7}{8}$") oil engine by J. och C. G. Bolinders Mekaniska Verksted, Stockholm. 91 nhp.
Post 1935 : 6-cyl. 2 S.C.S.A. ($10\frac{1}{2}$" x $13\frac{1}{2}$") oil engine by Crossley Brothers Ltd., Manchester. 116 nhp.
Post 1950 : 5-cyl. 2 S.C.S.A. ($10\frac{1}{2}$" x $13\frac{1}{2}$") oil engine by Crossley Brothers Ltd., Manchester, in 1949. 102 nhp.

11.1919 : Completed as **Warita** by I. J. Abdela & Mitchell Ltd., Queensferry, (Yard No. 404), for John Summers & Sons Ltd., Shotton. 1922 : Re-engined. 1935 : Re-engined. 1946 : Sold to Duff, Herbert & Mitchell Ltd., Liverpool, and renamed **Alfred Mason**. 1949 : Sold to Sir C. M. R. V. Duff, Bart. (Owen T. Williams, manager), Port Dinorwic. 1950 : Re-engined. 1952 : Sold to Duff, Herbert & Mitchell Ltd., (same managers), Port Dinorwic. 1953 : Sold to Dinorwic Slate Quarries Ltd., (same managers), Port Dinorwic. 10.1954 : Sold for £15,000, to J. Tyrrell & Sons, Arklow, Eire, but retained British flag. 3.1968 : Hammond Lane Foundry Ltd. commenced demolition at Dublin.

Alfred Mason is seen resting on the mud at Peel, Isle of Man on 3 August 1966.

(Author's collection/Roy Cripps)

Another photograph in the Isle of Man but the port is Douglas. The Tyronnall is seen on 19 August 1967. This photograph should be compared to that on page 7 and differences noted since the ship was modified.

(Author's collection/Roy Cripps)

T.2. *Tyrronall* (1966 - 1968)
O.N. 181511. 199g. 92n. - d. 107.0' x 23.1' x 8.9'.
Post 1939 : 244g. 122n. 330d. 128.3' x 23.1' x 8.5'.
4-cyl. 4 S.C.S.A. (270mm x 420mm) oil engine by Deutsche Werke A.G., Kiel. 44 nhp. 7.5 kts.

1935 : Completed by Lübecker Flender-Werke A.G., Lübeck Siems (Yard No.229), as the auxiliary 3-masted schooner *Heimat*, for Hugo Rubarth, Germany. 1939 : Lengthened. 5.1945 : Taken at Kiel as a war reparation by British Government, allocated to the Ministry of War Transport, (John Carter (Poole) Ltd., managers), and renamed *Empire Contamar*. 22.3.1947 : Dragged her anchor and grounded on rocks in St. Austell Bay, Cornwall, and was subsequently abandoned as being "not worth salvaging". She had been on a voyage from Maryport to Par with coal. Declared as a constructive total loss; she was purchased by John Tyrrell Ltd, Cardiff, as proxy for James Tyrrell, Ferrybank, Arklow. 6.1947 : Refloated, taken to the R. Clyde, rebuilt as a motor coaster, and renamed *Tyrronall*, registered at Cardiff. 1950 : Rebuilt and transferred to Dublin flag. 1968 : Sold to A. J. Gough, Hornchurch, retaining Dublin registry. 1973 : Sold to M. A. Smith, St. Peter Port, Guernsey and J. E. Fenton, Chagford, Devon, (Underwater Operations Company Ltd., managers), and converted into a salvage ship. 6.1974 : Reported as sold for demolition at Santander.

T.3. *Murell* (1) (1966 - 1972)
O.N. 400088. 319g. 163n. 390d. 133.8' x 24.7' x 7.5'.
As built : 6-cyl. 2. S.C.S.A. (10½"x 13½") oil engine by Crossley Brothers, Manchester. 115 nhp.
Post February 1943 : 6-cyl. 2 S.C.S.A. (265mm x 345mm) oil engine by Crossley Brothers, Manchester. 350 bhp.

9.5.1940 : Launched as *Fiddown* by Goole Shipbuilding & Repairing Company Ltd., Goole, (Yard No. 350), for S. Morris Ltd., Waterford, although vessel was registered at Goole. 7.1940 : Completed. 29.11.1940 : Run down and sunk by *HMS Campbeltown* when entering the River Mersey. 7.7.1942 : Subsequent to being raised, was beached at Tranmere. 10.7.1942 : Refloated, subsequently repaired, and re-engined. 1943 : Taken over by The Ministry of War Transport, London, (Craggs & Jenkins Ltd., Hull, managers), and renamed *Empire Estuary*. 1946 : Sold to E. J. & W. Goldsmith Ltd., London, and renamed *Goldfaun*. 1951 : Sold to Coastal Tankers Ltd., (Springwell Shipping Company Ltd., managers), London. 1952 : Sold to Short Sea Shipping Company Ltd., (same managers), London, and renamed *Creekdawn*. 7.1954 : Purchased by James Tyrrell, Arklow, and renamed *Murell*. 2.1972 : Sold for demolition to Hammond Lane Metal Ltd., Dublin. 3.1972 : Work completed.

*The trailer on the quayside in Dublin carries a bagged cargo which has been brought by the **Murell**.*

(Stan Tedford)

T.4. *Marizell*   (1966 - 1972)
O.N. 400138.   418g.   185n.   500d.   144.5' x 26.1' x 8.7'
6-cyl. 2 S.C.S.A. (250mm x 420mm) Polar type oil engine by Ab Atlas-Diesel, Stockholm. 465 bhp.

6.10.1947 : Launched as **A. R. Rawall** by Scheepswerf "Hoogezand" J. Bodewes, Hoogezand, (Yard No. 54), for Rederiet for m.s. A. R. Rawall, (R. N. Rawall, manager), Sweden. 2.1948 : Completed. 1956 : Sold to D. Fitzpatrick, Cobh, registered at Dublin, and later renamed **Kate**. (It was initially intended to rename **Jane**). 1959 : Purchased by James Tyrrell, Arklow, and renamed **Marizell**. 6.1972 : Sold to Psavadelis Evangelos & Sons, Greece, and renamed **Evagelistra Tinou**. 1975 : Sold to M. Theocharis and P. Andrianos, Greece, and renamed **Sea Thand VII**. 1977 : Sold to Stamatis Papadimitrou, Greece, and renamed **Dimitroula**. 1978 : Sold to unspecified Honduran owners and renamed **Ioanna II** and then **Dada**. 1995 : Having remained without a listed owner, *Lloyd's Register* deleted entry as continued existence was doubtful.

*The grey-hulled **Marizell** is seen at Dublin in June 1965.*

(Stan Tedford)

T.5. *Valzell* (1) (1966 - 1972)
O.N. 400353.   576g.   304n.   580d.   167.9' x 30.1' x 11.8'.
4-cyl. 2 S.C.S.A. (340mm x 570mm) Polar type, oil engine by British Auxiliaries Ltd., Glasgow. 125 nhp/300 bhp. 9.5 kts.

9.1935 : Completed as **Arbroath** by Caledon Shipbuilding & Engineering Company Ltd., Dundee, (Yard No. 347), for the Dundee, Perth & London Shipping Company Ltd., Dundee. 1962 : Purchased by James Tyrrell, Arklow, and renamed **Valzell** . 8.1972 : Sold to Haulbowline Industries Ltd., Cork, for demolition. 9.1972 : Work commenced.

*A splendid view of the **Valzell** at Cork in August 1965.*

(Stan Tedford)

7025310
T.6. **Darell** (1)   (1970 - 1974)
O.N. 400925.   387g. 223n. 517d.   136' 0" x 27' 6" x 11' 11"
6-cyl. 2 S.C.S.A. (220mm x 380mm), Brons 6GV-H vee type oil engine by Appingedammer Brons N.V., Appingedam.
600 bhp. 10.5 kts.

2.4.1970 : Keel laid by Verolme Cork Dockyard Ltd., Cork, (Yard No. 820), for James Tyrrell Ltd., Arklow. 7.7.1970 :
Launched. 1.11.1970 : Completed. 12.1974 : Sold to Marine Transport Services Ltd., Cork, and renamed **Carrigrennan**.
1989 : Sold to Woodrow J. Philpot, St. John's, Canada, and renamed **Free Trade**. 1994 : Sold to Hillier's Trades Ltd.,
Canada, and renamed **Mother Wood**. 2000 : Sold to Pierre Joreste, Port au Prince, Haiti, and transferred to Panama flag.
2004 : Still in existence.

Photographed at Dublin in July 1971, the Darell is the first vessel we see bearing the light green hull colour which has come to be a feature of Arklow ships, although the shades of green have varied over the years.

(Stan Tedford)

T.7. **Shevrell** (1)   (1971 - 1972)
O.N. 401055.   561g. 266n. 851d.   200' 0" x 29' 8" x 12' 0½"
6-cyl. 4 S.C.S.A. (330mm x 600mm) oil engine by N. V. Werkspoor Diesel, Amsterdam. 650 bhp. 10 kts.

5.1954 : Keel laid as **Huybergen** by Gebrouders van Diepen, Waterhuizen, (Yard No. 930), for The Government of the
Netherlands West Indies.   25.9.1954 : Launched as **Haaksbergen** for N. V. Zuid-Netherlandsche Scheepvaart
Maatschappij, Rotterdam, Netherlands. 20.11.1954 : Completed. 30.9.1958 : Sold to Zillah Shipping Company Ltd., (W.
A. Savage Ltd., managers), Liverpool, and renamed **Fernfield**. 31.12.1967 : Transferred to Coast Lines Ltd. 3.1971 :
Transferred to Coast Lines (Management) Ltd. 6.1971 : Transferred to Coast Lines (Services) Ltd. 1.10.1971 : P. & O.
Short Sea Shipping Ltd., appointed as managers. 8.12.1971 : Purchased by James Tyrrell Ltd., Arklow, and renamed
Shevrell. 4.1972 : Sold to Enterprise de Navigation de l'Isle Inc., Ile Aux Coudres, Charlevoix County, Canada, and
renamed **Coudres de l'Ile**. 15.6.1988 : Whilst on a voyage from Sept Iles to St. Catherines with scrap metal, in thick fog,
collided with **Algowest** (20,309g/82) off Pointe au Boisvert, St. Lawrence, and sank in a position 48.26N., 69.12W.

The original Shevrell was owned by James Tyrrrell for only a little over four months. Good colour photographs of her thus named are difficult to locate. However, we are pleased to be able to include a photograph of her flying the Canadian flag as Coudres de l'Ile. She is seen on the St Lambert Lock on the St Lawrence Seaway. Visible astern of her is the East Victoria Bridge which has been lowered to allow the passage of vehicles. All vessels tie up at the south wall of the lock which is a changeover point for pilots and is also a useful location for taking on stores.

(Author's collection)

The **Murell** is the second vessel in the fleet to bear this name. She is seen outward bound from Fowey.

(Author's collection)

5409380
T.8. **Murell** (2)   (1972 - 1974)
O.N. 401150.   1,110g. 602n. 1,483d.   202' 8" x 34' 9" x 18' 9"
Post 1996 : 571g. 427n. 1,507d.
6-cyl. 4 S.C.S.A. (385mm x 580mm) MaK 6M582AK type oil engine by Maschinenbau Kiel A. G., Kiel. 1,150 bhp. 11.5 kts.

17.5.1957 : Launched as **Ebba Robbert** by N. V., Scheepswerf Gebrouder van der Werf, Deest, (Yard No. 269), for Det. Dansk-Norsk Dampskibsselskab, (R. A. Robbert, manager), Denmark. 3.7.1957 : Completed. 1959 : Sold to Rederiet Seaway, (R. Fischer-Nielsen, manager), Denmark, and renamed **Stege**. 3.1963 : Sold to Coast Lines Ltd., Liverpool, and renamed **Terrier**. 1971 : Transferred to Coast Lines (Services) Ltd. 1.10.1971 : P & O Short Sea Shipping Ltd., appointed as managers. 7.4.1972 : Purchased by James Tyrrell Ltd., Arklow, and renamed **Murell** . 7.1974 : Sold to Nobleza Naviera S. A., Uruguay, and renamed **Quijote**. 1996 : Sold to Agroindustria Ara Poty S.r.L., Asuncion, Paraguay, and renamed **Omar G**, under the Paraguay flag.

T.9. **Arklow Vale** (1)   (1972) see ship No. M.5 in Arklow managed section.

The **Arklow Vale** in Belfast, with Coe's **Firethorn** astern of her.

(Stan Tedford)

T.10. **Shevrell** (2)   (1972 - 1973)
O.N. 401166.   881g. 384n. 1,112d.   203' 3" x 35' 9" x 14' 3"
6-cyl. 2 S.C.S.A. (360mm x 600mm) oil engine by Sulzer Brothers Ltd., Winterthur. 1,200 bhp. 12 kts.

17.7.1962 : Launched as **Wirral Coast** by Cammell, Laird & Company (Shipbuilders & Engineers) Ltd., Birkenhead, (Yard No. 1308), for Coast Lines Ltd., Liverpool. 31.8.1962 : Completed. 7.9.1962 : Delivered. 1971 : Transferred to Coast Lines (Services) Ltd. 1.10.1971 : P & O Short Sea Shipping Ltd. appointed as managers. 14.9.1972 : Purchased by James Tyrrell Ltd., Arklow, and renamed **Shevrell**. 7.1973 : Sold to Usborne & Son (London) Ltd., (Buries Markes Ltd., London, managers), London, and renamed **Portmarnock**. 1976 : G. T. Gillie & Blair Ltd., Newcastle, appointed as managers. 1977 : Sold to Taunos Shipping Corp., (Orb Shipping Company Ltd., London, managers). 1.1978 : Sold to Fulpass Ltd., (Usborne & Son [London] Ltd.), (G. T. Gillie & Blair Ltd., Newcastle, managers) to be renamed **Brookline**. 1979 : Sold, still as **Portmarnock**, to Khodor Itani, Peterborough, U.K., and renamed **Nadia 1**, under Lebanon flag. 1979 : Sold to Mrs. Nadia Hussein Mekkaoui, Lebanon. 27.11.1985 : Wrecked off Lebanon in heavy weather.

*Like the previous vessel of this name, the **Shevrell** (2), photographed at Plymouth on 17 March 1973, was also in the fleet only briefly.*
(Author's collection)

T.11. Bo Viking / Valzell (2)   (1973 - 1974)
O.N. 401235.   1,222g. 638n. 1,660d.   244' 4" x 37' 2" x 15' 4"
6-cyl. 4 S.C.S.A. (320mm x 450mm) oil engine by Motorenwerke Mannheim AG (MWM), Mannheim.

5.1966 : Launched as **Bo Viking** by Angyalfold Shipyard, Budapest, for Soren Pettersson, Sweden.   2.12.1966 : Completed. 1970 : Owner restyled Soren Pettersson Partrederi. 6.1973 : Purchased by James Tyrrell Ltd., Arklow, and subsequently renamed **Valzell**. 4.1974 : Sold to Bronze Shipping Ltd., London, and renamed **Jess** under the Cyprus flag. 1975 : Sold to Al-Karim Corp., Dubai, United Arab Emirates, and renamed **Freighter**, and registered at Dubai. 1977 : Renamed **Arabian Express**. 1978 : Sold to Silver Line Trading Corp., Dubai, United Arab Emirates, and renamed **Gulf Express**. 1982 : Demolished.

*Yet another vessel to spend only a short time in the fleet of James Tyrrell was the **Valzell** (2). She was photographed at St. Helier harbour, Jersey, on 12 October 1973.*

(Author's collection/D. Hocquard)

7368607

T.12. *Murell* (3)   (1974 - 1988)

O.N. 401312.   945g. 610n. 1,422d.   199' 8" x 32' 1" x 14' 0¼"

Post 1994 : 891g. 552n. 1,400d.

8-cyl. 4 S.C.S.A. (230mm x 270mm) MWM TBD440-8 type oil engine by Motorenwerke Mannheim A. G. (MWM), Mannheim. 1,080 bhp. 11 kts.

1972 : Ordered from Brattvåg Skipsinnredning & J. Johansens Sveiseverks, Brattvåg, (Yard No. 30), by Odfjell Rederi & Skips AS Frendo, Norway. 1973 : Contract taken over by James Tyrrell Ltd., Arklow. 3.1973 : Keel laid. 12.12.1973 : Launched. 6.1.1974 : Completed. 1988: Sold to Onesimus Dorey (Shipowners) Ltd., St. Peter Port, Guernsey, (James Fisher & Sons Public Limited Company, Barrow in Furness). 1988 : Bareboat chartered to Dennison Shipping Ltd., Kirkwall, and renamed **Hoxa Sound**. 3.1994 : Re-possessed following collapse of Dennison Shipping Ltd., Kirkwall. 9.1994 : Transferred to James Fisher & Sons Public Limited Company, Barrow in Furness, and subsequently to Onesimus Dorey (Shipowners) Ltd., St. Peter Port, Guernsey, and Wardwood Chartering Ltd., London, (Swinship Management B. V. Rotterdam, managers), and renamed **Teal I**, under the Bahamas flag. 1994 : Chartered to Northern & Mediterranean Shipping Ltd., Gibraltar, (same managers). 1996 : Unity Chartering (UCS) B.V., Ridderkerk, appointed as managers. 6.1997 : Sold to Alderney Shipping Company Ltd., St. Peter Port, Guernsey, and placed in a single ship company - Ortac Ltd., and renamed **Ortac** under the St. Vincent & the Grenadines flag. 2000 : Sold to Sambo Shipping S.A., Panama City, retaining flag and offered for resale. 12.2001 : Sold to Devon Shipping S. A., Rotterdam, and renamed **Margot** under the Panama flag. 2004 : Still in *Lloyd's Register*.

By contrast, the **Murell** (3) spent 14 years in the fleet. She is seen approaching Corpach on 4 August 1987.

(Bernard McCall)

The **Serenell** loads a bulk cargo by conveyor at Ipswich in October 1993.

(Stan Tedford)

T.13. **Valzell** (3)   (1976 - 1988) see ship No. A.10 in Arklow owned section.

T.14. **Serenell**   (1977 - 1995) see ship No. M.13 in Arklow managed section.

T.15. **Dorset Coast**   (1979)
1,206g. 626n. 1,360d.   220' 1" x 35' 10" x 14' 6½"
7-cyl. 2 S.C.S.A.(360mm x 600mm) Sulzer type oil engine by G. Clark & North Eastern Marine (Sunderland) Ltd., Sunderland. 1,260 bhp. 11.5 kts.

13.1.1959 : Launched by Ardrossan Dockyard Ltd., Ardrossan, (Yard No.427), for Coast Lines Ltd., Liverpool. 5.5.1959 : Completed. 1971 : Owners restyled Coast Lines (Services) Ltd. 1.10.1971 : P & O Short Sea Shipping Ltd., appointed as managers. 1.8.1972 : Transferred to Belfast Steamship Company Ltd., (same managers). 1.10.1973 : Transferred to General Steam Navigation (Trading) Ltd., (same managers). 31.3.1975: P & O Ferries Ltd., appointed as managers. 30.4.1976 : Transferred to P & O Ferries (General European) Ltd. 14.7.1978 : Transferred to P & O Ferries Ltd. 22.2.1979 : Sold to James Tyrrell Ltd., Dublin. 4.1979 : Sold to James S. T. Komiros, Egypt, and by him to Delta Marine Ltd., Egypt, and renamed **El Hussein**. 1980 : Owner restyled Delta Marine & Trading Ltd. 1981 : Sold to Omar Ibrahim, Saudi Arabia. 1981: Sold to Sayed Mohamed Sadaka Hitfa, Egypt, and renamed **El Kheer**. 1981 : Sold to Naviera Denton Venture S. de R. L., Gravesend, (Nialed Shipping Company Ltd., Gravesend, managers), and renamed **Denton Venture**, under the Honduras flag. 10.1982 : Intradis Shipping B.V., Rotterdam, appointed as managers. 1984 : Sold to Isabella Maritime Company, Piraeus, Greece, (Elvira Shipping Agency, managers), Greece, and renamed **Ourania**. 1985 : Sold to Brugse Scheepssloperij S. A., Belgium, for demolition. 24.6.1985 : Work commenced at Bruges.

*The **Dorset Coast** entered James Tyrrell's fleet in February 1979. Two months later she was sold to an Egyptian purchaser by whom she was renamed **El Hussein**, and it was under this name that she was photographed at Birkenhead on 13 May 1979.*

(Bernard McCall)

T.16. **Shevrell** (3)   (1981 - 1998) see ship No. M. 10 in Arklow managed section.

T.17. **Darell** (2)   (1982 - 1989) see ship No. M.31 in Arklow managed section.

T.18. **Arklow River** (2)   (1984 - 1987) see ship No. A.5 in Arklow owned section.

T.19. **Arklow Valley** (1)   (1984 - 1987) see ship No. A.6 in Arklow owned section.

T.20. **Arklow Glen**   (1988 - 1991) see ship No. M.15 in Arklow managed section.

T.21. **Arklow View** (1)   (1988 - 1990) see ship No. M.16 in Arklow managed section.

T.22. **Valzell** (3)   (1992 - 1996) see ship No. A.10 in Arklow owned section.

T.23. **Arklow Abbey**   (1995 - 1996) see ship No. A.3 in Arklow owned section.

T.24. **Arklow Spirit**   (1995 - 1998) see ship No. M.52 in Arklow managed section.

T.25. **Arklow Spray**   (1996 - 1998) see ship No. M.55 in Arklow managed section.

*There is no need for the crew of the **Arklow Spray** to close the hatch covers as the ship makes the short voyage from Immingham to Flixborough on 11 September 2000.*

(David Dixon)

Tyrrell Managed Vessels

TM.1. **Arklow Abbey**   (1981 - 1982) see ship No. A.3 in Arklow owned section.

TM.2. **Inisheer**   (1988 - 1990) see ship No. M.24 in Arklow managed section.

TM.3. **Inishowen** (1)   (1988 - 1990) see ship No. M.25 in Arklow managed section.

TM.4. **Inishfree** (1)   (1988 - 1990) see ship No. M.21 in Arklow managed section.

TM.5. **Arklow Valour**   (1995 -   ) see ship No. M.39 in Arklow managed section.

*The **Arklow Valour** leaves Llysfaen Jetty, Llanddulas, on 3 February 2000.*

(John P Evans)

Arklow Shipping Ltd
Arklow

A.1. *Arklow* (1970 - 1972)
O.N. 400850. 299g. 157n. 431d. 132.4' x 24.3' x 7.9'.
4-cyl. 4 S.C.S.A. (305mm x 450mm) oil engine by Motorenfabriek "De Industrie" D. & J. Boot, Alpen a/d Rijn. 240 bhp.
8.5 kts.

28.5.1948 : Launched as ***Banka*** by Scheepswerf "Voorwaarts", E. Hijlkema, Martinshoek, (Yard No. 153), for A. Boerma, Groningen, (N.V. Carebeka, Rotterdam, managers). 1948 : Completed. 1.1955 : Sold to Poromoka N. V., (M. Moerman, and P. Rogaar, managers), Rotterdam, and renamed ***Arctic***. 10.1958 : Sold to Partenreederei m.s."Herta II", (H. & D. Roesing, managers), Bremerhaven, West Germany, and renamed ***Herta II***. 1960 : Sold to Grave & Company, Bremerhaven. 3.1963 : Sold to Ulrich Liehr, Weserdeich, West Germany, and renamed ***Eisbar***. 1966 : Sold to D. Oltmann, Bremerhaven, West Germany. 1970 : Purchased by Arklow Shipping Ltd., Arklow, and renamed ***Arklow***. 20.11.1972 : Sold to Kendall Bros. (Portsmouth) Ltd., converted into a trailing suction dredger/sand carrier. 16.1.1973 : Renamed ***KB***. 20.12.1988 : Sold to Tollgate Medway (A. J. Philips), Rainham, Kent for demolition. 3.1.1989 : Arrived at Bloors Wharf.

*With interesting passenger ferries in the background, the Dublin-registered **Arklow**, with dark green hull, makes cautious progress through the port of Belfast in June 1970.*

(Stan Tedford)

A.2. *Arklow Bay* (1) (1971)
O.N. 401034. 533g. 264n. 851d. 183.3' x 29.6' x 10.7'.
8-cyl. 4 S.C.S.A. (290mm x 450mm) oil engine by Appingedammer Brons N.V., Appingedam. 500 bhp. 10 kts.

15.8.1953 : Launched as ***Medusa*** by Gebrouder van Diepen, Waterhuizen, (Yard No. 927), for Rederij Poseidon, (A. Kunst & J. Pekelder, managers), Groningen, Netherlands. 7.10.1953 : Completed. 11.1954 : Sold to Zillah Shipping Company Ltd., (W. A. Savage Ltd., managers), Liverpool, and renamed ***Fallowfield***. 31.12.1967 : Sold to Coast Lines Ltd. 1971 : Purchased by Arklow Shipping Ltd., (James Tyrrell), and renamed ***Arklow Bay***. 1971 : Sold to Bay Shipping Ltd., (Arklow Shipping Ltd., managers), Arklow. 22.9.1973 : Whilst on a voyage from Antwerp to Arklow with potash and other chemicals, suffered water ingress during a storm and was diverting to shelter in Milford Haven when she foundered 40 miles S. W. from St. Ann's Head, Pembrokeshire.

Arklow Bay *(1) leaving Londonderry whilst on charter to Anglo-Irish Transport Ltd, en route to Preston with containers.*

(W. J. Harvey)

8022626
A.3. **Arklow Abbey** (1981 - 1982)
O.N. 402218.   1,054g. 758n. 1,644d.   70,59m x 10,80m x 4,244m.
Post 1994 : 1,171g. 566n. 1,644d.
8-cyl. 2 S.C.S.A. (220mm x 380mm) Brons 8GV-H vee type, oil engine by Brons Industrie N.V., Appingedam, single reduction geared to screw shaft. 1,000 bhp. 11 kts.

1980 : Ordered by James Tyrrell Ltd. 7.1.1981 : Keel laid by Scheepswerf G. Bijlsma and Zonen B. V., Wartena, (Yard No. 615), for James Tyrrell Ltd. 30.10.1981 : Launched for Arklow Shipping Ltd., (James Tyrrell Ltd., managers), Arklow. 29.12.1981 : Completed. 1982 : Transferred to Bay Shipping Ltd., (Arklow Shipping Ltd., managers), Arklow. 1995 : Transferred to James Tyrrell Ltd and removed from management. 1996 : Sold to Fern Trading Ltd., Dublin, and renamed **Eastfern**. 1998 : Sold to Mideast Marine Ltd., and Fern Trading Ltd., (Fern Trading Ltd., Dublin, agents / F. T. Everard Management Ltd., London, freight managers). 8.2000 : Sold to associates of Anglo-Dutch Management Services Ltd., Woking, and renamed **Fern**, under the Honduras flag. 25.9.2000 : Whilst in ballast on passage from Montrose to Plymouth was damaged in a collision with **Kinsale** (5,306g/76) in the English Channel, 10 miles east of Dungeness. 2001 : Owners were recorded as Devo Shipping S. A., Panama City, under the Panama flag, and as being for re-sale. 2002 : Sold along with owning company Devo Shipping S. A., Panama City, to unspecified Venezuela-based owners, and renamed **Carmen Cecelia** under the Belize flag. Lloyd's Register (2004/2005) still lists vessel under this name but without an owner.

The **Arklow Abbey** at Barry on 13 November 1988.

(Bernard McCall)

The **Arklow Brook** (1) discharges wheat from Rouen at Sharpness on 12 March 1986.

(Cedric Catt)

A.4. **Arklow Brook** (1)   (1987 - 1988) see ship No. M.20 in managed section.

A.5. **Arklow River** (2)   (1987 - 1989) see ship No. M.14 in managed section.

A.6. **Arklow Valley** (1)   (1987 - 1991) see ship No. M.18 in managed section.

7366037
A.7. **Arklow Beach**   (1988 - 1989)
O.N. 402659.   3,642g. 2,251n. 5,482d.   102,29m (BB) x 15,75m x 6,928m.
Post 1995 : 3,663g. 2,153n. 5,482d.
8-cyl. 4 S.C.S.A. (381mm x 457mm) Mirrlees KMR-8 type oil engine by Mirrlees, Blackstone (Stockport) Ltd., Stockport.
4,500 bhp. 13.5 kts.

19.1.1976 : Keel laid as **Sandgate** by Appledore Shipbuilders Ltd., Appledore, (A.S.110), for Turnbull, Scott Shipping Company Ltd, London. 28.5.1976 : Launched. 8.7.1976 : Completed. 1982 : Sold to James Fisher and Sons PLC., Barrow in Furness, and renamed **Atlantic Fisher**. 1988 : Purchased by Arklow Shipping Ltd., and renamed **Arklow Beach**. 1989 : Sold to Sheil & Byrne (Overseas) Ltd., Dublin, (Arklow Shipping Ltd., managers). 1990 : Purchased by Arklow Shipping Ltd. 1992 : Sold to Sheil & Byrne (Overseas) Ltd., (Arklow Shipping Ltd., managers). 1994 : Transferred to Coastal Shipping Ltd., (same managers). 1995 : Sold to AS Hansen-Tangens Rederi, (H. E. Hansen, manager), Kristiansand, Norway, and renamed **Sunrana**. 1997 : Sold to AS Hansen-Tangens Rederi 3, (same manager), Kristiansand, Norway. 2002 : Sold to Sunrana AS., (Kopervik Ship Management AS., managers), Norway, under NIS flag. 2004 : Still in *Lloyd's Register*.

An unusual view of the **Arklow Beach** at Dublin on 20 September 1988 with Arklow crest on Fisher funnel colour.

(Author's collection / T. O'Connalain)

7204813
A.8. **Arklow River** (3)   (1989 - 1996)
O.N. 402663.   2,579g. 1,261n. 4,074d.   310' 6" (BB) x 46' 0" x 18' 10"
Post 1994 : 2,942g. 1,063n. 4,074d.
8-cyl. 4 S.C.S.A. (370mm x 400mm) Deutz RBV8M540 type oil engine by Klöckner Humboldt Deutz, Köln.   3,200 bhp.
13.5 kts. Thwartship thrust propeller forward.

Bulk cement carrier.
12.1971 : Keel laid as **Milburn Carrier** by J. J. Sietas GmbH & Co KG Schiffswerke, Hamburg, (Yard No. 704), for New Zealand Cement Holdings Ltd., Dunedin, New Zealand. 5.2.1972 : Launched. 6.4.1972 : Completed. 1989 : Purchased by Arklow Shipping Ltd., and renamed **Arklow River**. 1996 : Sold to Fantoft Cement K/S, Bergen, Norway, (Donnelly Shipmanagement Ltd., Limassol, Cyprus, managers), and renamed **Cem River** under the Norway NIS flag. 1999 : Sold to Fantoft Cement AS, (same managers), and transferred to St. Vincent & the Grenadines flag. 2000 : Tordenskjold Marine Gdynia Sp. Z.o.o., appointed as managers. 2004 : Sold to Jebsen Cement AS, Bergen, (Jebsen K.G., manager), Bergen, and renamed **Rhodos Cement**.

Arklow ships have long been regular callers to the Gloucestershire port of Sharpness carrying both import and export cargoes. The **Arklow River** (3) discharges a cargo of cement from Drogheda at Sharpness on 1 April 1990.

(Cedric Catt)

6600034
A.9. **Avoca** (1989 - 1990)
O.N. 402667. 161g. 95' 0" x 24' 11" x 10' 9"
8-cyl. 4 S.C.S.A. (8½"x 11½") Blackstone ETS-8 type oil engine by Lister, Blackstone & Company Ltd., Stamford, single reduction reverse geared to a single fixed pitch propeller operating within a Kort steerable nozzle. 850 bhp. 14 tonnes bollard pull. 10 kts.

Tug.

26.10.1965 : Launched as **Butegarth** by Richards (Shipbuilders) Ltd., Lowestoft, (Yard No. 483), for R. & J. H. Rea Ltd., London. 1.1966 : Completed. 1971 : Owner restyled as Cory Ship Towage Ltd. 1985: Owner restyled as Cory Towage Ltd. 1989 : Purchased by Arklow Shipping Ltd., and renamed **Avoca**. 1990 : Sold to Fluviais do Sado Limitida, Portugal, and renamed **Lutamar**, under Portugal registry. 28.9.1994 : Lloyd's Register classification withdrawn. 1995 : Owners restyled as Transportes Fluviais do Sado Lda. 2004 : Owners no longer listed in *Lloyd's Register*.

Avoca is the only tug to appear in the fleet. She was photographed on 3 September 1990.

(Author's collection/T. O'Connalain)

7416040
A.10. **Valzell** (3) (1990 - 1992)
O.N. 401547 1,038g. 569n. 1,608d. 61,52m x 10,42m x 4,776m.
Post 1994 : 999g. 488n. 1,608d.
6-cyl. 2 S.C.S.A. (220mm x 380mm) Brons 6TD200 vee type oil engine by N. V. Appingedammer Bronsmotorenfabriek, Appingedam. 1,200 bhp. 9.5 kts.

17.11.1975 : Keel laid by Verolme Cork Dockyard Ltd., Cork, (Yard No. 907), for James Tyrrell Ltd., Arklow. 16.3.1976 : Launched. 1.6.1976 : Completed. 1988 : Sold to Sheil & Byrne Ltd., Dublin. 1990 : Sold to Arklow Shipping Ltd. 1992 : Sold to James Tyrrell Ltd., (Arklow Shipping Ltd., managers). 1996 : Sold to Seawave Navigation Inc., (Vista Shipping Agency, Tallinn, managers), and renamed **Skylark**, under the St. Vincent & the Grenadines flag. 2004 : Still in *Lloyd's Register*.

*About to pass the popular vantage point at Eastham, the **Valzell** heads towards the Manchester Ship Canal on 30 June 1979.*

(Bernard McCall)

The **Arklow Beach** was photographed on 26 October 1989, with cranes removed.

A.11. **Arklow Beach**   (1990 - 1992) see ship No. A.7 above.

A.12. **Arklow View** (1)   (1990 - 1991) see ship No. M.15 in managed section.

A.13. **Arklow Spray**   (1998 -   ) see ship No. M.49 in managed section.

A.14. **Arklow Spirit**   (1998 -   ) see ship No. M.46 in managed section.

The hull of the **Arklow Spirit** as she nears completion at the builder's yard appears to be a slightly different shade of green from that in the photograph on page 33. Other photographs of S class ships being built will be found on page 70.

9238399
A.15. **Arklow Rose** (2) (2002 -)
O.N. 403332. 2,999g. 1,635n. 4,530d. 89,99m x 14,18m x 5,68m.
8-cyl. 4 S.C.S.A. (200mm x 300mm) MaK 6M25 type oil engine by Krupp MaK Maschinenbau GmbH, Kiel, single reduction reverse geared to screw shaft with controllable pitch propeller. 1,849 bhp. 11.5 kts. Thwartship thrust propeller forward.

Multi-purpose cargo-vessel with 138 TEU container capacity. 102 hold/36 deck.
10.2000 : Ordered from Schps. & Mfbk Barkmeijer Stroobos B. V., Stroobos, (Yard No. 299), for Arklow Shipping Ltd.
15.3.2001 : Keel laid. 17.12.2001 : Launched. 10.2.2002 : Completed.

This book includes several illustrations of Arklow ships in the River Mersey or on the Manchester Ship Canal. These ships are regularly to be seen sailing to and from Cerestar Wharf in Manchester and it was here that the **Arklow Rose** was photographed on 13 April 2004 as she discharged maize from Bordeaux. Cargoes are generally loaded at either Bordeaux or Bayonne, or less frequently at Tonnay Charente. Having discharged their maize at Cerestar, the ships often load scrap at Irwell Park Wharf on the Canal, a cargo which they deliver to northern Spain, thus becoming available to load more maize for Cerestar at a French Bay port.

(Jordan Seifarth)

9287302
A.16. **Arklow Wave** (2003 -)
O.N. 403336. 8,938g. 4,815n 13,988d. 136,4m (BB) x 21,25m x 8,35m.
6-cyl. S.C.S.A. (380mm x 475mm) Wärtsilä 6L38B type oil engine by Wärtsilä-Finland Oy, Finland, reduction geared to controllable pitch propeller. 5,438 bhp. 13.5 kts. Bow thrust unit forward.

29.5.2003 : Keel laid by Kyokuyo Zosen K. K., Shimoneseki / Chofu, (Yard No. 447), for Arklow Shipping Ltd. 11.8.2003 : Launched. 5.11.2003 : Completed.

9287766
A.17. **Arklow Resolve** (2004)
O.N. 403337. 2,999g. 1,369n. 4,500d. 89,9m x 14,15m x 5,68m.
8-cyl. 4 S.C.S.A. (200mm x 300mm) MaK 8M20 type oil engine by Krupp MaK Maschinenbau GmbH, Kiel, single reduction reverse geared to screw shaft with controllable pitch propeller. 1,849 bhp. 12.5 kts. Thwartship thrust propeller forward.

Multi-purpose cargo-vessel with 138 TEU container capacity. 102 hold/36 deck.
2003 : Ordered from Schps. & Mfbk Barkmeijer Stroobos B. V., Stroobos, (Yard No. 302), for Arklow Shipping Ltd.
7.2.2003 : Keel laid. 31.10.2003 : Launched. 11.1.2004 : Completed. 2.2004 : Sold to Invermore Shipping Ltd., Dublin, (Arklow Shipping Ltd., managers).

Another view of Cerestar Wharf. On this occasion it was the **Arklow Resolve** that was discharging on 7 August 2004. She had arrived from Bordeaux two days earlier. As suggested on page 31, she proceeded to load scrap for Pasajes at the nearby Irwell Park Wharf.

(Roy Cressey)

At the time of writing only two W-class vessels are in service. The **Arklow Wave** is seen in the Shannon estuary on 27 August 2004 heading to the aluminium factory at Aughinish to load for Straumsvik in Iceland.

(Barry Standerline)

Once again Llysfaen Jetty is the location. Loading of the limestone cargo is well underway in this photograph of the **Arklow Spirit** taken in April 1996.

(Stan Tedford)

A reminder of the days when many quaysides were rail served. Lansing Bagnall shunter No. **DL2** positions wagons as required alongside the **Arklow Dawn** (1) which loads steel coils for Antwerp. The date is 16 April 1981, and the port is Sharpness.

(Cedric Catt)

M.1. Arklow Bay (1)   (1971 - 1973) see ship No. A.2 in owned section.

7368994
M.2. Arklow Dawn (1)   (1973 - 1987)
O.N. 401310.   943g.   629n. 1,420d.   60,91m x 9,56m x 4,310m.
Post 1995 : 939g.   636n.   1,443d.
As built : 8-cyl. 4 S.C.S.A. (220mm x 280mm) Deutz RSBA8M528 type oil engine by Klöckner Humboldt Deutz, Köln, geared to a controllable pitch propeller. 1,160 bhp. 11kts.
Post 1983 : Reported as having been refitted with a MAN M9 type engine. 1,080 bhp.

6.1972 : Keel laid as **Frendo Annemor** by Johan Drage AS., Rognan, (Yard No. 370), for Skips AS Frendo, Norway. 4.9.1973 : Launched as **Annemor**. 14.11.1973 : Purchased by Bay Shipping Ltd. 5.12.1973 : Completed as **Arklow Dawn** for Vale Shipping Ltd., (Arklow Shipping Ltd., managers). 6.1987 : Sold to Capricorn AS., (Rolf Gresdal, manager), Farsund, Norway, and renamed **Kimare**. 7.1987 : Transferred to Norway NIS registry. 12.1988 : Sold to Frei Shipping AS, Kristiansund, Norway, and renamed **Frei Mignon**. 1990 : Sold to Atlantic Bulk AS, Kristiansund, Norway, and renamed **Atlantic Fosna**. 1990 : Sold to O. S. Shipping S. de R. L., Honduras, (O. P. Svenssons Skeppsmakleri AB, Gothenburg, managers), and renamed **Salona** under the Honduras flag. 2004 : Still in *Lloyd's Register*.

*The **Arklow Dawn** was back at Sharpness on 14 January 1984, this time loading barley for Dundalk.*

(Cedric Catt)

M.3. Arklow Bridge (1)   (1976 - 1977)
O.N. 401535. 367g. 231n. 635d.   171' 6" x 27' 10" x 10' 6"
5-cyl. 2 S.C.S.A. (230mm x 400mm) Alpha 405-23 type oil engine by Alpha Diesel AS., Frederikshavn. 300 bhp. 10 kts.

7.3.1963 : Launched as **Jørgen Priess** by Solvesborgs Varv AB., Solvesborg, (Yard No. 64), for Tage Priess, Denmark. 25.4.1963 : Completed. 1971 : Sold to Jorn Moller Partrederei, Denmark. 1974 : Sold to Timber Carriers Ltd., London, and renamed **Timber Skipper**. 30.12.1975 : Purchased by Vale Shipping Ltd., (Arklow Shipping Ltd., managers). 1976 : Renamed **Arklow Bridge**. 1977 : Sold to Lydiabourne Ltd., Rochester, (London & Rochester Trading Ltd., Strood, commercial managers), and renamed **Jostrica**, under the Republic of Ireland flag. 9.1981 : Sold to N. E. Murray and placed under Maritime Shipping and Towage Company, Queenborough. 1982 : Sold to Pineapple Bay Inc., (N. E. Murray, Queenborough, manager), under the Panama flag. 7.6.1985 : Departed Wisbech for Hamburg but suffered machinery damage and arrived Lowestoft next day. 4.7.1985 : Left Lowestoft for Queenborough in tow of tug **Jaygo**. Repairs uneconomical and vessel laid up at Queenborough (same owners / manager). 4.1990 : On settlement of insurance claim, vessel sold to N. E. Murray (Marine Contractors) Ltd., Queenborough and by 4.1991 had been demolished.

*The first **Arklow Bridge** was another vessel to spend only a short time with the company. Managed by Arklow Shipping Ltd, she is seen outward bound in the River Ouse.*

(Charles Hill)

5402066

M.4. *River Avoca* (2) (1976 - 1977)
O.N. 401550.   299g. 171n. 575d.   154' 7" x 28' 11" x 10' 2"
5-cyl. 2 S.C.S.A. (230mm x 400mm) Alpha 405-23 type oil engine by Alpha Diesel AS., Frederikshavn. 350 bhp. 9.5 kts.
Post 1970 : 4-cyl. 2 S.C.S.A. (260 x 400mm) Alpha 404-26VO type oil engine by Alpha Diesel AS., Frederikshavn.
400 bhp. 9.5 kts.

21.10.1963 : Launched as *Mistralen* by Sønderborg Skibsværk, Sønderborg, (Yard No. 40), for P. O. Kristian Jacobsen, Denmark. 16.1.1964 : Completed. 1966 : Sold to H. P. Cleemann Partrederi, Denmark, and renamed *Hathershus*. 1970 : Re-engined. 1971 : Sold to Carsten Brebol, Denmark, and renamed *Leise Nova*. 1976 : Sold to Ole Andrup-Jakobsen Partrederi, Denmark, and renamed *Ceresio*. 6.1976 : Sold to Vale Shipping Ltd., (Arklow Shipping Ltd., managers), and renamed *River Avoca*. 7.1977 : Sold to Clyde Port Authority, subsequently restyled as Clyde Port Ltd., Glasgow, and converted into a buoy tender. 1978 : Renamed *Torch*. 1997 : Sold to Poole Harbour Commissioners, Poole. 21.7.1997 : Towed from Greenock by the tug *Chief R*. 24.7.1997 : Arrived at Poole for conversion into a floating accommodation vessel for visiting yachtsmen at Poole Marina. However that was not undertaken. 2001 : Sold to Labrador Shipping Ltd., (Anglo Dutch Management Services Ltd., Woking, managers), and was subsequently laid up at Portland and Oreston. 2003 : Sold to a private individual for possible conversion to a nightclub, but remains in lay-up at Portland.

M.5. *Arklow Vale* (1) (1977 - 1981)
O.N. 401164.   443g. 219n. 620d. 166' 10" x 27' 1" x 10' 9¹/₄"
8-cyl. 2 S.C.S.A. (220mm x 380mm) Brons 8GH-H vee type, oil engine by Appingedammer Brons, Appingedam. 500 bhp.
11 kts.

23.11.1962 : Launched as *Roscrea* by Scheepsbouw "Hoogezand" J. Bodewes, Hoogezand, (Yard No.110), for the Limerick Steamship Company Ltd., Limerick. 15.3.1963 : Completed. 1964 : Sold to J. & A. Davidson Ltd., Aberdeen, and renamed *Torquay*. 9.1972 : Purchased by James Tyrrell Ltd., Arklow, and renamed *Arklow Vale*. 12.1972 : Sold to Marine Transport Services Ltd., Cobh, and renamed *Glenbrook*. 5.1977 : Purchased by Vale Shipping Ltd., (Arklow Shipping Ltd., managers), Arklow, and reverted to *Arklow Vale*. 9.1981 : Sold to Concord Leasing Ltd., Brentford, (Bankside Shipping and Towing Company Ltd., mortgagees), retaining Dublin registry. 1984 : A. Petherick, Bude, and Others became mortgagees.   1985 : Renamed *Golden Vale*. 1985 : Sold to Rulespeed Ltd., Southam, (A. Petherick, Bude, and Others). 30.8.1985 : Laid up at Ipswich. 2.1986 : Sold to Spice Island Coastal Shipping Ltd., Portsmouth, (Salama Shipping Ltd., Ealing, managers), and renamed *Rehema*, under the Tanzania flag. 1.9.1986 : Whilst on delivery voyage from Bilbao to Dar-es-Salaam, suffered machinery problems and was abandoned by her crew 80 miles S.E. of Socotra, and subsequently foundered.

Although of indifferent technical quality, this view of the **Arklow Vale** *(1) discharging wheat for the mill / bakery at Milford, Mulroy Bay, County Donegal, on 27 July 1980 still merits inclusion.*

(Author's collection)

A fine view of the Dutch-built **Arklow Vale** *(1) at Belfast.*

(Stan Tedford)

6810847
M.6. *Arklow Bridge* (2)   (1977 - 1978)
O.N. 401736.   500g. 317n. 833d.   189' 3" x 29' 9" x 11' 6"
6-cyl. 2 S.C.S.A. (220mm x 380mm) Brons 6GB type, oil engine by Appingedammer Brons, Appingedam. 560 bhp.
10 kts.

28.2.1968 : Launched as *Constance* by Scheepswerf "Voorwaarts", Martinshoek, (Yard No. 198), for Wijnne and Barends B. V., Rotterdam. 24.4.1968 : Completed. 10.1977 : Purchased by Vale Shipping Ltd., (Arklow Shipping Ltd., managers), Arklow, and renamed *Arklow Bridge*. 1978: Removed from management. 8.1981 : Sold to Carisbrooke Shipping Ltd., Isle of Wight, and renamed *Mark C*, retaining Republic of Ireland flag. 1986 : Sold to Harris & Dixon (Shipbrokers) Ltd., London, (Carisbrooke Shipping PLC, Isle of Wight, managers), and renamed *Courtfield*, retaining Republic of Ireland flag. 1991 : Sold to Ocean Research & Recovery Ltd., under the Turks & Caicos Islands (UK) flag. 1995 : Sold to R. J. Guilo Properties, Belize, and renamed *Briana*. 1996 : Sold to Allround Shipping & Trading Inc., Belize, and renamed *Solution*.   1996: Renamed *Sea Boekanier*. 3.1997 : Foundered.

Red hulls are not associated with Arklow ships, but the **Arklow Bridge** (2) retained hers after purchase from Dutch owners. She is seen at Runcorn in September 1979.

(Danny Kelliher)

Another view of the red-hulled **Arklow Bridge** (2), this time at Arklow on 24 July 1978.

(Author's collection/T. O'Connalain)

*The lights on the quayside and on the ships are shining brightly indicating that it was late in the evening when the **Arklow Day** (1) was emerging from the lock at Sharpness at the start of a voyage to Arklow on 27 July 1979.*

(Cedric Catt)

6710839
M.7. **Arklow Day** (1) (1978 - 1979)
O.N. 401856.   400g. 243n. 800d.   172' 7" x 32' 3" x 11' 2"
Post 1994 : 522g. 223n. 800d.
6-cyl. 4 S.C.S.A. (270mm x 400mm) Callesen 6-427-FOT type oil engine by Aabenraa Motorenfabriek, Heinrich Callesen AS, Aabenraa, geared to a controllable pitch propeller. 690 bhp. 11kts

12.1966 : Keel laid as **Knudsvig** by Sønderborg Skibsværft, Sønderborg, (Yard No. 53), for Rus Shipping, Denmark. 10.3.1967: Launched for Sønderjydsk Rederi AS., (P. F. Cleemann, managers), Aabenraa, Denmark. 26.6.1967 : Completed. 1970 : Sold to Steen E. Høffner Partrederi, (Eric Høffner, manager), Copenhagen, Denmark, and renamed **Nordic Proctor**. 1975 : Sold to Diamond Fertilizer and Chemical Company Ltd., London, (Fred Parkes Shipping Company Ltd., Grimsby, managers), and renamed **Nordic Clover**. 8.1978 : Sold to Bay Shipping Ltd., Arklow, (Arklow Shipping Ltd., managers), and renamed **Arklow Day**. 1979 : Removed from management. 5.1980 : Sold to AS Rovde Sandfrakt, Rovde / Ålesund, Norway, and renamed **Rodfjell**. 1998 : Sold to Rodfjell AS., Rovde. 2000 : Sold to Rovde Supply AS., Rovde, Norway, (Rovde Shipping AS., managers), and fitted as a self-discharging vessel. 2001 : Sold to Follafrakt AS., Steinsdalen, Norway, and renamed **Stig Halle**. 2004 : Still in *Lloyd's Register.*

6916902
M.8. **Arklow River** (1) (1979 - 1982)
O.N. 401967.   400g. 255n. 713d.   158' 1" x 28' 10" x 12' 1"
Post 1995 : 485g. 247n. 713d.
6-cyl. 2 S.C.S.A. (220mm x 380mm) Brons 6GV-H vee type oil engine by Appingedammer Brons, Appingedam. 450 bhp. 10 kts.

17.4.1969 : Launched as **Apollo 1** by N. V. Bodewes Scheepswerven, Martinshoek, (Yard No. 501), for Rederij m.s. Apollo 1, (Beck's Scheepvaartkantoor N. V., managers), Netherlands. 20.6.1969 : Completed. 11.1979 : Sold to Vale Shipping Ltd., (Arklow Shipping Ltd., managers), Arklow, and renamed **Arklow River**. 5.1982 : Sold to J. & W. P. Crews Company Ltd., Sharpness, (same managers), and renamed **Cynthia June**. 2.1986 : Sold to Tora Sea Services Ltd., Douglas, Isle of Man, (M. & H. Shipping Ltd., Douglas, managers), and renamed **Tora**. 1988 : Sold to Mezeron Ltd., Isle of Man, and renamed **Greeba River**. 2.1997 : Sold to Raymond Burton Berkshire, Arnold's Cove, Canada, and renamed **Placentia Sound**. 2004 : Still in *Lloyd's Register.*

*Still looking every inch a Beck coaster with grey hull and white letter B on her bow, the **Arklow River** (1) awaits her turn to discharge alfalfa pellets from Rotterdam after arriving at Sharpness on 27 January 1980.*

(Cedric Catt)

8022822
M.9. **Arklow Castle** (1)   (1981 - 1992)
O.N. 402183.   1,054g. 757n. 1,640d.   70,59m x 10,80m x 4,23m.
Post 1983 : 1,895g. 971n. 3,033d   83.75m.
8-cyl. 2 S.C.S.A. (220mm x 380mm) Brons 8GV-H vee type, oil engine by Brons Industrie N.V., Appingedam, single reverse reduction geared to screw shaft. 1,000 bhp. 11 kts.

7.1.1981 : Keel laid by Scheepswerf "Ferus Smit" B.V., Foxhol, (Yard No. 227), for Bay Shipping Ltd. Arklow. 28.8.1981 : Launched for Arklow Shipping Ltd.   21.10.1981 : Completed for Vale Shipping Ltd., Arklow, (Arklow Shipping Ltd., managers). 1983: Lengthened. 30.11.1992 : Whilst outward from France to London, wrecked about 1 mile north of Sables d'Olonne, her hull later breaking into two pieces.

*The **Arklow Castle** (1) arrives at Barry in March 1986 with a cargo of grain for Rank's Atlantic Mill.*

(P C Olsen)

*Another Rank's mill, this time Solent Mill in Southampton, is the setting for this photograph of the **Shevrell** (3) on 28 August 1983.*

(Bernard McCall)

8022602
M.10. **Shevrell** (3)   (1981 - 1998)
O.N. 402215.   1,393g. 1,029n. 2,691d.   75,37m x 12,60m x 5,168m.
Post 1991 : 1,895g. 971n. 3,033d.   83.75m x 12.60m x 5.168m.
12-cyl. 2 S.C.S.A. (220mm x 380mm), Brons 12GV-H vee type, oil engine by Brons Industrie N.V., Appingedam, single reduction reverse geared to a screw shaft. 1,500 bhp. 11.5 kts.

7.1.1981 : Keel laid by Niestern Sander B.V., Delfzijl, (Yard No. 506), for Bay Shipping Ltd. Arklow. 19.9.1981 : Launched for James Tyrrell Ltd.   24.10.1981 : Completed, Arklow Shipping Ltd. appointed as managers.   1991 : Lengthened. 20.1.1998 : Sold to AS Garibaldi, (Tordenskjold Rederi AS, Bergen, managers), and renamed **Garibaldi** under the Norway NIS flag.   1999 : Sold to Penny Hope Company Ltd., (Storesund Management AS., Haugesund, managers), under the Cyprus flag. 2000 : Managers restyled as Tordenskjold Marine Haugesund AS. 2001 : Sold to Garibaldi Shipping AS (same managers). 2004 : Sold to Mody Shipping Company S.A.R.L., Beirut, and renamed **Ghofran** under the Lebanon flag.

*Photographed in surprisingly strong winter sunlight, the **Arklow Abbey** loads a cargo of wheat for Rotterdam at Sharpness on 22 December 1982.*

(Cedric Catt)

M.11. **Arklow Abbey**   (1982 - 1996) see ship No. A.2 in owned section.

M.12. **Cynthia June**   (1982 - 1986) see ship No. M.8 above.

Arklow Abbey in the French port of Le Légue in August 1995. Note the addition of a travelling gantry crane.

(Author's collection)

The **Cynthia June** arrives at Teignmouth on 17 April 1985.

(Bernard McCall)

8500575
M.13. **Serenell** (1983 - 1995)
O.N. 401619. 1,038g. 596n. 1,632d. 61,52m x 10,42m x 4,776m.
6-cyl. 2 S.C.S.A. (220mm x 380mm) Brons 6TD200 vee type oil engine by B.V., Motorenfabriek "De Industrie", Alpen a/d Rijn. 1,200 bhp. 9½ kts.

16.10.1976 : Keel laid by Verolme Cork Dockyard Ltd., Cork, (Yard No. 909), for James Tyrrell Ltd., Arklow. 12.2.1977 : Launched. 19.5.1977 : Completed. 1983 : Arklow Shipping Ltd. appointed as managers. 1995 : Sold to Ominar Shipping Company Ltd., Blackrock, Co. Dublin, and renamed **Fiona May** under Cyprus flag. 1996 : McKenna Marine Services Ltd., Dublin, appointed as managers. 4.2003 : Sold to associates of Drenth Ship Consult, Istanbul, and renamed **Maya** under the Antigua and Barbuda flag. 2004 : Sold to Inka International Trading & Shipping N.V., (Inka Denizcilik ve Tasimacilik Ticaret Ltd., Sirketi (Inka Shipping & Transport Company Ltd), Istanbul, managers), and renamed **Core** under the Antigua and Barbuda flag.

The **Serenell** sets out from Kinsale on 13 July 1995.

(Aubrey Dale)

On 14 September 1984, the **Arklow River** (2) was at Sharpness loading wheat bran pellets for discharge in Cork.

(Cedric Catt)

7424035
M.14. **Arklow River** (2) (1984 - 1987)
O.N. 402318. 1,394g. 990n. 2,711d. 71,48m x 13,03m x 5,722m.
Post 1996 : 1,399g. 867n. 2,711d.
6-cyl. 4 S.C.S.A. (320mm x 420mm), MaK 6M453AK type oil engine by MaK Maschinenbau GmbH, Kiel. 2,000 bhp.
13 kts.

5.12.1975 : Launched as **Atlantic Coast** by Ørskov's Staalskibsværft I/S., Frederikshavn, (Yard No. 84), for Hans J. Therkildsen, Næstved, Denmark. 30.3.1976 : Completed. 1979 : Sold to James Fisher & Sons Ltd., Barrow in Furness, and renamed **Bay Fisher**. 7.1984 : Purchased by James Tyrrell Ltd., (Arklow Shipping Ltd., managers), Arklow, and renamed **Arklow River**. 1987 : Purchased by Arklow Shipping Ltd. 1989 : Sold to Vidalia Finance S. A., Panama, and renamed **Arklowe River**. 1990 : Renamed **Northstar**. 1991 : Sold to Sea Cross Shipping & Chartering Ltd., Honduras, and renamed **Bay Fish**. 1992 : Sold to International Marine Management Company Ltd., United Arab Emirates, and renamed **Yusr**. 1994: Lloyd's Register deleted owners. 1996 : Owners now listed as Blue Sky Shipping & Trading Company, Sharjah, United Arab Emirates, and renamed **Nabil**. 2004 : Still in Lloyd's Register.

7716488
M.15. **Arklow View** (1) (1984 - 1991)
O.N. 402322. 993g. 671n. 1,519d. 65,82m x 10,80m x 4,303m.
Post 1994 : 1,094g. 583n. 1,519d.
6-cyl. 4 S.C.S.A. (320mm x 450mm), MaK 6M452AK type oil engine by MaK Maschinenbau GmbH, Kiel. 1,200 bhp.
10.25 kts.

15.3.1978 : Keel laid as **Terona** by Scheepswerf Bijlholt B. V., Foxhol, (Yard No. 604), for J. Vermaas Scheepvaartbedrijf B. V., Rotterdam, (Veerenigde Scheepvaartbedrijf V. S. B., Rotterdam, managers). 25.8.1978 : Launched. 20.10.1978 : Completed. 8.1984 : Purchased by Viewglen Ltd., Arklow (Arklow Shipping Ltd., managers), Arklow, and renamed **Arklow View**. 1988 : Sold to James Tyrrell Ltd., and Arklow Shipping Ltd., (same managers). 1990 : Sold to Arklow Shipping Ltd. 9.1991 : Transferred to James Tyrrell Ltd., & Arklow Shipping Ltd., (Arklow Shipping Ltd., managers), and renamed **Arklow Dew** to release the name for a new vessel. 1992 : Sold to Vale Shipping Ltd., Arklow, (same managers). 1994 : Sold to AS Ami, Nordnes, (Misje Offshore Marine AS, Bergen, managers), Norway, and renamed **Nautilus**. 1999 : Sold to Fritind AS, Kopervik, and renamed **Fritind**, under the Bahamas flag. 5.2.2000 : Kopervik Ship Management AS, Kopervik, Norway, appointed as managers. 2004 : Still in Lloyd's Register.

The **Arklow View** (1) was photographed at Dublin on 15 September 1986.

(Author's collection/
T. O'Connalain)

7716490
M.16. **Arklow Glen** (1984 - 1994)
O.N. 402321. 993g. 671n. 1,519d. 65,82m x 10,80m x 4,319m.
Post 1994 : 1,094g. 583n. 1,519d.
6-cyl. 4 S.C.S.A. (320mm x 450mm), MaK 6M452AK type oil engine by MaK Maschinenbau GmbH, Kiel. 1,200 bhp.
10.5 kts.

5.9.1978 : Keel laid as **Tromp** by Scheepswerf Bijlholt B. V., Foxhol, (Yard No. 605), for J. Vermaas Scheepvaartbedrijf B. V., Rotterdam, (Veerenigde Scheepvaartbedrijf V. S. B., Rotterdam, managers). 18.5.1979 : Launched. 4.7.1979 : Completed. 8.1984 : Purchased by Viewglen Ltd., Arklow, (Arklow Shipping Ltd., managers), Arklow, and renamed **Arklow Glen**. 1988 : Purchased by James Tyrrell Ltd., (same managers). 9.1991 : Transferred to James Tyrrell Ltd., & Arklow Shipping Ltd., (same managers). 1992 : Sold to Vale Shipping Ltd., Arklow, (same managers). 1994 : Sold to Fortuna AS, Nordnes, (Misje Offshore Marine AS, Bergen, managers), Norway, and renamed **Fortuna** under the Bahamas flag. 2004: Managers restyled Misje Rederi AS, Bergen.

*Outward bound in the New Waterway on 4 August 1984, the **Arklow Glen** had been acquired only very recently. Her funnel is in the process of being painted and her upperworks remain in the colours of her previous Dutch owners.*

(Author's collection/L. Bosschart)

*Now in full Arklow livery, the **Arklow Glen** is seen at Barry in early January 1989.*

(Bernard McCall)

7405091

M.17. **Arklow Bridge** (3)   (1984 - 1990)

O.N. 402329.   1,592g. 1,049n. 3,147d.   79,51m (BB) x 13,62m x 5,538m.

8-cyl. 4 S.C.S.A. (320mm x 450mm) MaK 8M452AK type oil engine by MaK Maschinenbau GmbH, Kiel. 2,004 bhp.
12 kts.

Ice-strengthened general cargo vessel with a 72 TEU container capacity.

2.10.1975 : Keel laid as **Cairncarrier** by Martin Jansen GmbH & Co KG, Schiffswerk u Motorenfabrik, Leer, (Yard No. 134), for Shaw, Savill & Albion Company Ltd., London. 5.12.1975 : Launched. 3.2.1976 : Completed. 1982 : Sold to Tequila Maritime S.A., Panama, and renamed **Tequila Sunset**. 1984 : Purchased 50:50 by Sheil & Byrne Ltd., Dublin, and Arklow Shipping Ltd., (Arklow Shipping Ltd., managers), Arklow, and renamed **Arklow Bridge**. 1988 : Sold to Sheil & Byrne Overseas Ltd., Dublin, (same managers). 1990: Sold to Boterita Shipping S.A., (Navimar S.A., Lugano, Switzerland, managers), and renamed **Wave Rose**, under the Panama flag. 1990 : Removed from management. 1993 : Sold to Samer Maritime Ltd., St. Vincent, (Successors Shipping S.A., Piraeus, managers), and renamed **Armour**, retaining Panama flag. 1997 : Sold to Night Flare Navigation S. A., Piraeus, (Sigma Maritime Inc., managers), and renamed **Eurolink**, retaining Panama flag. 2000 : Sold to unspecified Panama flag owners (International Maritime Services, managers). 2004 : Still in Lloyd's Register.

The **Arklow Bridge** (3) at Dublin 10 December 1984.

(Author's collection/T. O'Connalain)

7633612

M.18. **Arklow Valley** (1)   (1984 - 1987)

O.N. 402411.   1,398g. 869n. 2,453d.   66,53m x 13,19m x 5,201m

Post 1980 : 1,597g. 1,053n. 2,703d.   73,34m x 13,19m x 5,087m.

Post 1996 : 1,707g. 920n. 2,703d.

8-cyl. 4 S.C.S.A. (320mm x 480mm) MWM TBD484-8 type oil engine by Motorenwerke Mannheim, (MWM), Mannheim.
1,485 bhp. 11 kts.

6.4.1977 : Keel laid as **Procyon** by Scheepswerf Bodewes Gruno, Foxhol, (Yard No. 240), Moerman Libra Shipping B.V., Schiedam, Netherlands. 24.6.1977 : Launched. 29.8.1977 : Completed for Kustvaartbedrijf Moerman B.V., Schiedam, Netherlands. 1980 : Lengthened. 1984 : Purchased by James Tyrrell Ltd., (Arklow Shipping Ltd., managers), Arklow, and renamed **Arklow Valley**. 1987 : Purchased by Arklow Shipping Ltd. 1991 : Sold to Onesimus Dorey (Shipowners) Ltd., St. Peter Port, Guernsey, (James Fisher & Sons Public Limited Company, Barrow in Furness), renamed **Rockpoint**, and bareboat chartered to Dundalk Shipowners Ltd. 1996 : Renamed **Solway Fisher**, James Fisher & Sons (Liverpool) Ltd., appointed as managers. 1999 : Sold to James Fisher & Sons (Liverpool) Ltd., (James Fisher (Shipping Services) Ltd., managers). 2001 : Sold to Capricorn Shipping Company Ltd., (Alpha Shipping Agency Ltd., Riga, managers), and renamed **Solvita**, under the St Vincent and the Grenadines flag. 2004 : Still in Lloyd's Register.

*The **Arklow Valley** (1) underway at sea.*

(Stan Tedford)

7022239
M.19. **Bermudiana**   (1985 - 1987)
O.N. 339928.   1,578g. 892n. 2,181d.   279' 11" x 45' 3" x 15' 5"
6.cyl. 4 S.C.S.A. (410mm x 470mm) Werkspoor 6TM410 type oil engine by Stork-Werkspoor Diesel B. V., Amsterdam, geared to a controllable pitch propeller. 3,200 bhp. 16 kts.

Fixed-guide containership with a 124 TEU capacity. 48 hold/76 deck (inc. 33 refrigerated)
19.6.1970 : Launched as **Tamega** by A. Vuijk & Zonen's Scheepswerven N. V., Capelle a/d IJssel (Yard No. 850), for Sea Containers Ltd., (J. B. Sherwood, manager), London. 9.1970 : Completed. 1974 : Renamed **City of Genoa**, and removed from management. 1982 : Transferred to Hustler 2 Ltd., and renamed **Hustler Ebro**, under Bermuda flag. 1983 : Transferred to Sea Containers Ltd., and renamed **Bermudiana**. 1984 : Transferred to Seaco Holdings Ltd., (Sea Management Services (S.M.S.), managers). 19.8.1985 : Arrived at Holyhead and placed in lay-up. 28.8.1985 : Arklow Shipping Ltd., appointed as managing agents whilst remaining in lay-up. 1987: Sold to associates of James Tyrrell Ltd., Arklow. 17.1.1987 : Departed Holyhead en route to Dublin towed by the tug **Afon Goch**. 1987 : Sold to Minart Corporation, Fort Lauderdale, and renamed **Minart**, under the Honduras flag. 19.5.1987 : Sailed from Dublin for Miami. 1988 : Renamed **Anita**. 1988 : Renamed **Prince Hamlet**. 1989 : Renamed **Lloyd Bermuda II**. 1989 : Sold to Excelsior Navigation Company Ltd., Limassol, Cyprus, (Interorient Navigation Company Ltd., Limassol, Cyprus, managers), and renamed **Zim Levant**, under the St. Vincent & The Grenadines flag. 1992 : Sold to Atlantic Gulf Shipping Company Ltd., Limassol, and renamed **Jason**, under the Cyprus flag. 1992 : Renamed **Idmon**. 1993 : Transferred to St. Vincent & the Grenadines flag. 1993 : Sold to Filippos Shipping Company S. A., Piraeus, and renamed **Filippos**, under St. Vincent & the Grenadines flag. 1995 : Filippos Shipping Company appointed as managers. 1996 : Sold to Avante S.r.L., Asuncion, Paraguay. 2004 : Still in *Lloyd's Register.*

*The **Bermudiana** at Dublin on 20 January 1987.*

(Author's collection/ T. O'Connalain)

7405065

M.20. *Arklow Brook* (1)   (1985 - 1987)

O.N. 402422.   1,534g. 998n. 3,195d.   79,51m (BB) x 13,62m x 5,55m.

Post 1995 : 1,770g. 1,042n. 3,195d.

8-cyl. 4 S.C.S.A. (320mm x 450mm) MaK 8M452AK oil engine by Atlas-MaK Maschinenbau GmbH, Kiel. 2,004 bhp.
12 kts.

Ice-strengthened general cargo vessel with a 72 TEU container capacity.

2.7.1974 : Keel laid as *Cairnliner* by Martin Jansen GmbH, & Co KG, Schiffswerke u Motorenfabrik, Leer, (Yard No. 131), for Shaw, Savill & Albion Company Ltd., London. 21.10.1974 : Contract sold to Ph. Van Es, Rotterdam, Netherlands. 2.11.1974 : Launched as *Breezand*. 21.1.1975 : Completed. 1983 : Sold to Matapan Shipping Inc., (Van Ommeren Marine Management Ltd., London, managers), and renamed *Aramis*, under the Greece flag. 8.1985 : Transferred to Irish flag, and renamed *Arklow Brook*, (Arklow Shipping Ltd., managers). 1987 : Purchased by Arklow Shipping Ltd. 1988 : Sold to KS Framvaren, Farsund, Norway, (Vindhall Shipping AS, Farsund, agents), and renamed *Framvaren*. 1993 : Sold to Marine Eagle S. A., (Th. K. Skoufos & Company, Piraeus), (Alkionis II Shipping Company, Piraeus, managers), Panama, and renamed *Stathis G*. 2000 : Sold to Hornet S.A., (same managers), under St. Vincent & the Grenadines flag. 2004 : Still in *Lloyd's Register*.

Arklow Brook (1) *in the Solent in August 1986.*

(Colin Drayson)

Arklow Vale (2) *makes good speed as she heads up the River Scheldt in 1986.*

(Author's collection/L. Bosschaart)

7811410
M.21. *Arklow Vale* (2) (1985 - 1988)
O.N. 402427. 1,599g. 1,053n. 2,703d. 73,41m x 13,21m x 5,10m.
Post 1994 : 1,707g. 920n. 2,703d.
8-cyl. 4 S.C.S.A. (320mm x 480mm) MWM TBD484-8 type oil engine by Motorenwerke Mannheim, (MWM), Mannheim. 1,450 bhp. 11 kts.

15.8.1979 : Keel laid as *Capricorn* by Scheepswerf Bodewes Gruno B.V., Foxhol, (Yard No. 243), for Kustvaart-Bedrijf Moerman B. V., Schiedam, Netherlands. 21.9.1979 : Launched. 17.10.1979 : Completed. 1985 : Purchased 50:50 by Sheil & Byrne Ltd. and Arklow Shipping Ltd., (Arklow Shipping Ltd., managers), Arklow, and renamed *Arklow Vale*. 1988 : Sold to Sheil & Byrne (Overseas) Ltd., (same managers). 1988 : Sold to Coastal Shipping Ltd. (James Tyrrell Ltd., managers), and renamed *Inishfree*. 1990 : Arklow Shipping Ltd. appointed as managers. 1994 : Sold to Lakehead Shipping Ltd., Gibraltar, (Thomas Watson (Shipping) Ltd., managers), Rochester, and renamed *Lady Sylvia* under the Bahamas flag. 1999 : Sold to Taurus Maritime Company Ltd, (Alpha Shipping Agency Ltd., Riga, Latvia, managers), and renamed *Elvita*, under the Malta flag. 2004 : Still in *Lloyd's Register*.

8713809
M.22. *Arklow Manor* (1987 - 2000)
O.N. 402422*. 1,523g. 643n. 1,722d. 73,84m x 11,51m x 3,814m.
Post 1994 : 1,524g. 783n. 2,181d. 73,84m x 11,51m x 4,383m.
6-cyl. 4 S.C.S.A. (240mm x 330mm) MaK 6M332AK type oil engine by Krupp MaK Maschinenbau GmbH, Kiel, reverse geared to screw shaft. 1,018 bhp. 11.5 kts. Thwartship thrust propeller forward.

Ice-strengthened general cargo vessel, strengthened for heavy cargoes and with a 31 TEU container capacity.
22.12.1987 : Completed by Schiffswerft Hugo Peters, Wewelsfleth, (Yard No. 634), for Arklow Shipping (Overseas) Ltd., (Arklow Shipping Ltd., managers), Arklow. 1992 : Official Number altered to 402573. 9.2000 : Sold to Arabian Tanker Company Llc, (BR Marine Consult AS, Copenhagen, managers), and to be renamed *Copernicus* under the Liberia flag. Subsequently taken to Poland for conversion into a chemical tanker. 2001 : Upon completion of conversion, was sold to Euro Shipping Ltd., Panama, (same managers). 2004 : Still in *Lloyd's Register*.

* In 1992 it was realised that an official departmental error had allocated the same number to *Arklow Brook* (1) q.v.

*The hatch covers are being closed on the **Arklow Manor** after completion of loading her limestone cargo at Llysfaen Jetty, Llanddulas, on 26 March 2000.*

(John P Evans)

8314548

M.23. **Arklow Rose** (1)   (1987 - 1990)
O.N. 402496.   4,292g. 1,777n. 4,515d.   102,49m x 17,56m x 5,501m.
6-cyl. 4 S.C.S.A. (450mm x 550mm) MaK 6M551AK oil engine by Krupp MaK Maschinenbau GmbH, Kiel, single reduction geared to screw shaft. 3,800 bhp. 13 kts.

Ice-strengthened general cargo vessel with a 326 TEU container capacity. 140 hold/186 deck.
2.12.1983 : Keel laid as **Faroe Trader** by Ørskov Christensens Staalskibs AS., Frederikshavn (Yard No. 129), for P/f., Faroe Trader, Copenhagen, (Knud I. Larsen, Copenhagen, manager), Denmark. 2.3.1984 : Launched. 28.6.1984 : Completed. 1987 : Purchased by Capstan Shipping Ltd., Arklow, (Arklow Shipping Ltd., managers), and renamed **Arklow Rose**. 1988 : Sold to Aedha Enterprises Ltd., Arklow, (same managers). 1990 : Sold to Compagnie Meridionale de Navigation & Navale Transports Vinicoles LEDUC S. A., Montpellier, France, and renamed **Cygne**. 1996 : Sold to France Euro Tramp (Fr.E.T.) S.A., Montpellier, France. 1997 : Renamed **Fret Aquitaine**, French Antarctic Territory flag. 1999 : Sold to Rho 7 Beta Ltd., Port Moresby, Papua New Guinea, (Consort Express Lines Pty. Ltd., Papua New Guinea, managers), and renamed **Gazelle Coast**. 2004 : Still in *Lloyd's Register*.

*Then the largest vessel in the Arklow fleet and the largest to have had Arklow as port of registry, the **Arklow Rose** (1) is seen in the New Waterway.*

(Author's collection/Jim Prentice)

8416786

M.24. **Inisheer** (1988 - 1995)
O.N. 402583.   1,839g. 946n. 2,194d.   78,01m x 12,70m x 4,25m.
Post 2002 : 1,850g. 950n. 2,440d.   78,63m x 12,70m x 4,68m.
10-cyl. 2 S.C.S.A. (190mm x 350mm) oil engine by "Bolnes" Motorenfabriek B.V., Krimpen a/d Lek. 1,700 bhp. 10 kts. Thwartship thrust propeller forward.
Post 1988 : 6-cyl. 4 S.C.S.A. (240mm x 330mm), MaK 6M332AK type oil engine by Krupp MaK Maschinenbau GmbH, Kiel. 1,767 bhp. 10 kts.

Ice-strengthened general cargo vessel, with a 124 TEU container capacity. 62 hold/62 deck.
2.8.1984 : Keel laid by Tille Scheepsbouw B. V., Kootstertille, (Yard No. 246), for G. Wessels, West Germany. 21.12.1984 : Launched as **Elisa von Barssel** for m.s. "Elisa von Barssel" Norbert Kroger, Barssel, West Germany. 22.4.1985 : Completed. 1985 : Renamed **Flagship 1**. 1986 : Sold to Navic Schifffahrtskontor, Haren-Ems, (Gerhard Wessels, Haren-Ems, manager), West Germany, and renamed **Lia Ventura**. 1988 : Purchased by Coastal Shipping Ltd., Arklow, (Arklow Shipping Ltd., managers), Arklow, and renamed **Inisheer**. 1988 : James Tyrrell Ltd. appointed as managers. 6.1988 : Re-engined. 1990 : Arklow Shipping Ltd. appointed as managers. 1995 : Renamed **Dunkerque Express**. 1999 : Reverted to **Inisheer**. 4.2.2002 : Sold to Rederiet M. H. Simonsen ApS, Svendborg, Denmark, and renamed **Oraness**, under the Denmark (DIS) flag, and subsequently converted into an edible oil tanker. 2004 : Still in *Lloyd's Register*.

*The **Inisheer** was photographed as she departed from Cowes and entered the Solent on 22 May 2001.*

(Brian Ralfs)

As noted elsewhere, the **Inisheer** was an ideal multipurpose vessel. On page 9, we saw her working on a container service from the Manchester Ship Canal. In the above photograph, she leaves Irlam Locks on 6 November 1988 heading to Cerestar Wharf with a cargo of maize. She was an infrequent visitor in this trade.

(Bernard McCall)

8121719
M.25. **Inishowen** (1)   (1988)
O.N. 402658.   1,236g.   679n.   3,126d.   77,02m x 13,04m x 5,50m.
Post 1994 : 1,988g. 1,075n. 3,126d.
8-cyl. 4 S.C.S.A. (240mm x 330mm) MaK 8M332AK type oil engine by Krupp MaK Maschinenbau GmbH, Kiel. 1,750 bhp. 10 kts.

16.3.1982 : Keel laid as **Raimundo A** by Astillieros Luzuriaga S. A., Pasajes, (Yard No. 227), for Artaza y Compania S. A., Pasajes, Spain. 30.12.1982 : Launched. 22.6.1983 : Completed. 1988 : Purchased by Coastal Shipping Ltd., Arklow, (Arklow Shipping Ltd., managers), Arklow, and renamed **Inishowen**. 1988 : James Tyrrell Ltd. appointed as managers. 1990 : Arklow Shipping Ltd. appointed as managers. 1.12.1995 : Sold to Paal Wilson & Company AS, Haugesund, Norway, (Continental Ship Management AS, Karmsund, Norway, managers), and renamed **Grimo**, under the Bahamas flag. 23.8.2001 : Transferred to Wilsons Shipowning II AS, Bergen, (Wilson Ship Management (Bergen) AS, managers), retaining Bahamas flag. 2004 : Still in *Lloyd's Register.*

The **Inishowen** photographed at Ghent on 17 June 1995.

(Martin Penwright)

M.26. **Inishfree** (1)   (1988 - 1994) see ship No. M.21. above.

8713811
M.27. **Arklow Bay** (2)   (1988 - 2004)
O.N. 402586.   1,523g.   643n.   1,722d.   73,85m x 11,80m x 3,81m.
Post 1994 : 1,524g.   783n.   2,181d.
6-cyl. 4 S.C.S.A. (240mm x 330mm) MaK 6M332AK type oil engine by Krupp MaK Maschinenbau GmbH, Kiel, reverse geared to screw shaft. 1,018 bhp. 11.5 kts. Thwartship thrust propeller forward. Tunnel thruster unit.

Ice-strengthened general cargo vessel, strengthened for heavy cargoes and with a 31 TEU container capacity.
2.12.1987 : Keel laid as **Arklow Mansion** by Schiffswerft Hugo Peters, Wewelsfleth, (Yard No. 635), for Arklow Shipping Ltd. 20.2.1988 : Launched as **Arklow Bay**. 29.3.1988 : Completed for Arklow Shipping (Overseas) Ltd., (Arklow Shipping Ltd., managers). 2004 : Sold to Austrheim Frakt AS (Knut Saetre og Sonner, Austrheim, Norway, managers); renamed **Frakt** and transferred to St Vincent & the Grenadines flag.

*A picturesque view of the **Arklow Bay** at Mistley in March 1990.*

(Stan Tedford)

*The **Arklow Marsh**, whose builder's yard number follows immediately after that of the **Arklow Bay**, at Garston on 29 September 2001. Following their sale out of the Arklow fleet, both of these vessels have been purchased by the same Norwegian owner.*

(David Williams)

8713823
M.28. **Arklow Marsh**   (1988 - 2004)
O.N. 402656.   1,523g. 643n. 1,722d.   73,84m x 11,80m x 3,814m.
Post 1994 : 1,524g. 783n. 2,181d.
6-cyl. 4 S.C.S.A. (240mm x 330mm) MaK 6M332AK type oil engine by Krupp MaK Maschinenbau GmbH, Kiel, reverse geared to screw shaft. 1,018 bhp. 11.5 kts. Thwartship thrust propeller forward.

Ice-strengthened general cargo vessel, strengthened for heavy cargoes and with a 31 TEU container capacity.
1.2.1988 : Keel laid by Schiffswerft Hugo Peters, Wewelsfleth, (Yard No. 636), for Arklow Shipping (Overseas) Ltd.
23.4.1988 : Launched (Arklow Shipping Ltd. managers). 26.5.1988 : Completed. 2004 : Sold to Fehn Bereederungs GmbH & Co KG (Fehn Schiffahrts GmbH & Co KG, Leer, managers); renamed **Fehn Trader** and transferred to Antigua & Barbuda flag.

*Having arrived four days earlier from Nordenham, the **Arklow Mill** heads down the Thames to Iceland on 7 August 1992. At this date, she was fitted with a deck gantry.*

(Author's collection/G. R. Wise)

A strong evening sun highlights the **Arklow Mill** as she makes her way up the River Trent on 23 May 2001.

(Roy Cressey)

8800157
M.29. **Arklow Mill**   (1988 - 2004)
O.N. 402660.   1,523g.   643n.   1,740d.   73,84m x 11,80m x 3,814m.
Post 1994 : 1,524g.   783n.   2,181d.
6-cyl. 4 S.C.S.A. (240mm x 330mm) MaK 6M332AK type oil engine by Krupp MaK Maschinenbau GmbH, Kiel, reverse geared to screw shaft. 1,018 bhp. 11.5 kts. Thwartship thrust propeller forward.

Ice-strengthened general cargo vessel, strengthened for heavy cargoes and with a 31 TEU container capacity.
21.4.1988 : Keel laid by Schiffswerft Hugo Peters, Wewelsfleth, (Yard No. 637), for James Tyrrell Ltd. 6.8.1988 : Launched. 13.9.1988: Completed for Arklow Shipping (Overseas) Ltd., (Arklow Shipping Ltd., managers). 2004 : Sold to Falkeid Shipping A/S, Finnøy, Norway; renamed **Falknes** and transferred to Bahamas flag.

The **Arklow Vale** (3) was anchored in the Solent on 3 July 2004.

(Bernard McCall)

8822040

M.30. **Arklow Vale** (3) (1989 -   )
O.N. 402661.   2,867g. 1,596n. 4,250d.   88,20m x 13,66m x 5,81m.
8-cyl. 4 S.C.S.A. (240mm x 330mm) MaK 8M332AK type oil engine by Krupp MaK Maschinenbau GmbH, Kiel, single reduction reverse geared to screw shaft. 1,767 bhp. 11 kts. Thwartship thrust propeller forward.

Ice-strengthened general cargo vessel, strengthened for heavy cargoes and with a 173 TEU container capacity. 105 hold/68 deck.
22.9.1988 : Keel laid by Schiffswerft Hugo Peters, Wewelsfleth, (Yard No. 625), for Invermore Shipping Ltd., Dublin.
10.12.1988 : Launched (Arklow Shipping Ltd., managers). 20.1.1989 : Completed.

8022614

M.31. **Inishark** (1989 - 1997)
O.N. 402221.   1,504g. 971n. 2,691d.   77,40m x 12,51m x 6,25m.
Post 1986 : 1,895g. 971n. 3,033d.   83,75m x 12,60m x 5,168m.
Post 1998 : 2,099g. 1,145n. 3,033d.   83,75m x 12,60m x 5,168m.
As built : 12-cyl. 2 S.C.S.A. (220mm x 380mm) Brons 12GV-H vee type, oil engine by Brons Industrie N. V., Appingedam. 1,475 bhp. 11.5 kts.
Post 1999 : 9-cyl. 4 S.C.S.A. (240mm x 260mm) Kromhout 9FHD240G type oil engine by Stork-Wärtsilä Diesel B.V., Zwolle. 1,903bhp.

7.1.1981 : Keel laid as **Darell** by Scheepswerf Bijlholt B. V., Foxhol, (Yard No. 612), for Arklow Shipping Ltd. 20.11.1981 : Launched. 13.1.1982 : Completed for James Tyrrell Ltd., (Arklow Shipping Ltd., managers), Arklow. 1986 : Lengthened.   1989 : Transferred to Coastal Shipping PLC., Arklow, (same managers), and renamed **Inishark**. 1997 : Sold to Salina Shipping Ltd., Malta, (Strand Shipping A.S., Mo-i-Rana, Norway, managers) and renamed **Salina** under Malta flag. 1998 : Rune Jakobsens Rederi AS., Mo-i-Rana, appointed as managers. 1.1999 : Re-engined. 2004 : Still in *Lloyd's Register.*

Inishark in the River Thames on 10 April 1993.
(Author's collection/K. Allen)

M.32. **Arklow Beach** (1989 - 1990) see ship No. A.6. in owned fleet section.

7529079

M.33. **Eve Rita** (1989 - 1991)
O.N. 402566.   427g. 252n. 690d.   45,55m x 8,34m x 3,247m.
As built : 6-cyl. 4 S.C.S.A. (222mm x 292mm) ES6 type oil engine by Mirrless Blackstone (Stamford) Ltd., Stamford. 468 bhp. 10 kts.
Post 1990 : 6-cyl. 4 S.C.S.A. (210mm x 300mm) Stork DRO16K type engine by Stork-Wärtsilä Diesel B. V., Zwolle. 503 bhp.

28.4.1976 : Keel laid as **Gainsborough Miller** by J. W. Cook & Company (Wivenhoe) Ltd., Wivenhoe, (Yard No. 1452) for Channel Coasters Ltd. (the shipping division of Spillers Ltd., London. 7.12.1976 : Launched. 15.3.1977 : Completed.   1981 : Sold to Crescent Shipping Ltd., Rochester, Kent, (London & Rochester Trading Company Ltd.,) and renamed **Westerence**. 1987 : Sold to Cerecoal Chartering Ltd., Dublin, and renamed **Eve Rita**. 1989 : Sold to Arklow Shipping (Coastal) Ltd., (Arklow Shipping Ltd., managers). 9.1990 : Re-engined. 1991 : Sold to Morgan Diesel & Engineering Ltd., Dublin, and renamed **Mantan**.   1992 : Renamed **Avoca**. 1993 : Sold to Société des Etablissements Pajarola et Compagnie, Les Sables d' Olonne France, and renamed **Casam III**. 6.10.1993 : Irish registry closed. 2004 : Still in *Lloyd's Register.*

The **Eve Rita** approaches Great Yarmouth.

(Darren Green)

*Not the most attractive of vessels when viewed from her stern quarter, the **Eve Rita** is seen at Dundalk with hull painted in a different shade of blue from that in the photograph on the previous page.*

(Jim Brodigan)

8906779
M.34. **Arklow Victor** (1989)
O.N. 402662.   2,827g. 1,596n. 4,250d.   88,20m x 13,66m x 5,81m.
8-cyl. 4 S.C.S.A. (240mm x 330mm) MaK 8M332AK type oil engine by Krupp MaK Maschinenbau GmbH, Kiel, single reduction reverse geared to screw shaft. 1,767 bhp. 11 kts. Thwartship thrust propeller forward.

Ice-strengthened general cargo vessel, strengthened for heavy cargoes and with a 173 TEU container capacity. 105 hold/68 deck.

24.11.1988 : Keel laid by Schiffswerft Hugo Peters, Wewelsfleth, (Yard No. 626), for Invermore Shipping Ltd., Dublin. 8.4.1989 : Launched, (Arklow Shipping Ltd., managers). 18.5.1989 : Completed. 17.12.1989 : Whilst on a voyage from Bayonne to Manchester, capsized and sank at a position 47.37N., 4.47W.

*The **Arklow Victor** capsized and sank only seven months after her delivery. (It has since been suggested that the vessel may have struck an undetected underwater obstacle and suffered hull penetration)*

She was photographed in the River Trent on 5 June 1989.

(Author's collection/Charles Hill)

9003524
M.35. **Arklow Viking** (1990 - 2000)
O.N. 402665.   2,827g. 1,595n. 4,261d.   88,20m x 13,68m x 5,79m.
8-cyl. 4 S.C.S.A. (240mm x 330mm) MaK 8M332AK type oil engine by Krupp MaK Maschinenbau GmbH, Kiel, single reduction reverse geared to screw shaft. 1,767 bhp. 11 kts. Thwartship thrust propeller forward.

Ice-strengthened general cargo vessel, strengthened for heavy cargoes and with a 173 TEU container capacity. 105 hold/68 deck.
4.7.1989 : Keel laid by Schiffswerft Hugo Peters, Wewelsfleth, (Yard No. 627), for Invermore Shipping Ltd., Dublin.
19.12.1989 : Launched, (Arklow Shipping Ltd., managers). 24.1.1990 : Completed. 1.2000 : Sold to Forester Shipping Company Ltd., (Brise Schiffahrts GmbH, Hamburg, managers), and renamed **Forester** under the Antigua & Barbuda flag.
2001 : Managers restyled as Brise Bereederungs GmbH & Co KG.

Orb Jetty, also known as Lysaght's Wharf, on the River Usk at Newport was established to export finished steel products. The closure of the nearby Llanwern steel works in 2002 seemed to seal the fate of the jetty but in fact it remains in use, ironically for the import of steel. It was, however, an export cargo being taken to Bilbao by the **Arklow Viking** on 7 March 1999.

(Cedric Catt)

8912481
M.36. **Arklow Meadow**   (1990 - 2000)
O.N. 402666.   1,523g. 643n. 1,747d.   73,84m x 11,51m x 3,803m.
Post 1994 : 1,524g. 783n. 2,181d.
6-cyl. 4 S.C.S.A. (240mm x 330mm) MaK 6M332AK type oil engine by Krupp MaK Maschinenbau GmbH, Kiel. 1,018 bhp. 11.5 kts. Thwartship thrust propeller forward.

Ice-strengthened general cargo vessel, strengthened for heavy cargoes and with a 31 TEU container capacity.
21.7.1989 : Keel laid by J. G. Hitzler, Schiffswerft u Maschinenfabrik, Lauenburg, (Yard No. 794), for Arklow Shipping Ltd.
7.2.1990 : Launched for Sailaway Sailor PLC., (Arklow Shipping Ltd., managers). 20.3.1990 : Completed. 1995 : Transferred to Arklow Shipping (Overseas) Ltd., (same managers). 4.2000 : Sold to Frakto AS, Austrheim, Norway, (Knut Saetre og Sonner, Austrheim, managers), and renamed **Frakto** under the St. Vincent & the Grenadines flag.

The **Arklow Meadow** in the River Neath on 20 May 1998, bound for Giants Wharf, Briton Ferry, to load crushed slag for Drogheda.

(Bill Moore)

9003536
M.37. **Arklow Venture** (1)   (1990 - 2000)
O.N. 402668.   2,827g. 1,595n. 4,261d.   88,20m x 13,66m x 5,79m.
8-cyl. 4 S.C.S.A. (240mm x 330mm) MaK 8M332AK type oil engine by Krupp MaK Maschinenbau GmbH, Kiel, single reduction reverse geared to screw shaft. 1,767 bhp. 11 kts. Thwartship thrust propeller forward.

Ice-strengthened general cargo vessel, strengthened for heavy cargoes and with a 173 TEU container capacity. 105 hold/68 deck.
20.12.1989 : Keel laid by Schiffswerft Hugo Peters, Wewelsfleth, (Yard No. 628), for Invermore Shipping Ltd., Dublin.
7.3.1990 : Launched   (Arklow Shipping Ltd., managers). 5.5.1990 : Completed. 1.2000 : Sold to Thruster Shipping Company Ltd., (Brise Schiffahrts GmbH, Hamburg, managers), and renamed **Thruster** under the Antigua & Barbuda flag.
2001 : Managers restyled as Brise Bereederungs GmbH & Co KG. 2004 : Still in *Lloyd's Register.*

On 12 April 1994, the **Arklow Venture** has just passed Old Quay Swing Bridge at Runcorn on her way to Manchester. Later in that same year, on 1 December, this ship had the honour of sailing past Her Majesty the Queen on the occasion of the opening of the new Parkway Bridge near Cerestar Wharf.

(Bernard McCall)

8912493
M.38. **Arklow Moor**   (1990 - 2004)
O.N. 402669.   1,523g. 643n. 1,732d.   73,85m x 11,77m x 3,813m.
Post 1994 : 1,524g. 774n. 2,165d.
6-cyl. 4 S.C.S.A. (240mm x 330mm) MaK 6M332AK type oil engine by Krupp MaK Maschinenbau GmbH, Kiel. 1,018 bhp. 11.5 kts. Thwartship thrust propeller forward.

Ice-strengthened general cargo vessel, strengthened for heavy cargoes and with a 31 TEU container capacity.
4.9.1989 : Keel laid by J. G. Hitzler, Schiffswerft u Maschinenfabrik, Lauenburg, (Yard No. 795), for Arklow Shipping Ltd.
30.6.1990 : Launched for Arklow Shipping (Overseas) Ltd., (Arklow Shipping Ltd., managers). 1.8.1990 : Completed.
2004 : Sold to Fehn Bereederungs GmbH & Co KG (Fehn Schiffahrts GmbH & Co KG, Leer, managers); renamed **Fehn Broker** and transferred to Antigua & Barbuda flag.

9015046
M.39. **Arklow Valour**   (1990 - 1995) & (1996 -   )
O.N. 402670.   2,827g. 1,595n. 4,299d.   88,20m x 13,61m x 5,81m.
8-cyl. 4 S.C.S.A. (240mm x 330mm) MaK 8M332AK type oil engine by Krupp MaK Maschinenbau GmbH, Kiel, single reduction reverse geared to screw shaft. 1,767 bhp. 11 kts. Thwartship thrust propeller forward.

Ice-strengthened general cargo vessel, strengthened for heavy cargoes and with a 173 TEU container capacity.
105 hold/68 deck.
2.1990 : Keel laid by Schiffswerft Hugo Peters, Wewelsfleth, (Yard No. 629), for Invermore Shipping Ltd., Dublin.
11.8.1990 : Launched (Arklow Shipping Ltd., managers). 9.9.1990 : Completed. 1995 : Transferred to Coastal Shipping PLC, (James Tyrrell Ltd., managers). 1996 : Arklow Shipping Ltd. appointed as managers.

The **Arklow Moor** was a rare visitor to Royal Portbury Dock, Bristol, on 5 July 2004. She arrived on the morning tide with a cargo of forest products from Antwerp and sailed to Newport on the evening tide of the same day.

(Kevin Jones)

Arklow Valour is outbound in the River Usk on 27 March 1999.

(Danny Lynch)

M.40. *Inishowen* (1) (1990 - 1995) see ship No. M.25. above.

9031430
M.41. *Arklow Villa* (1991 - 2002)
O.N. 402672. 2,827g. 1,595n. 4,258d. 88,25m x 13,68m x 5,802m.
8-cyl. 4 S.C.S.A. (240mm x 330mm) MaK 8M332AK type oil engine by Krupp MaK Maschinenbau GmbH, Kiel, single reduction reverse geared to screw shaft. 1,767 bhp. 11 kts. Thwartship thrust propeller forward.

Ice-strengthened general cargo vessel, strengthened for heavy cargoes and with a 173 TEU container capacity.
105 hold/68 deck.
5.10.1990 : Keel laid by Schiffswerft Hugo Peters, Wewelsfleth, (Yard No. 633), for Invermore Shipping Ltd., Dublin.
13.4.1991 : Launched. 28.5.1991 : Completed, (Arklow Shipping Ltd., managers). 25.2.2002 : Sold to m.s. "Wilster" Schiffahrtsges. mbH & Co KG, Hamburg, (Brise Bereederungs GmbH & Co KG, Hamburg, managers), and renamed *Wilster*, under the Antigua & Barbuda flag.

*The **Arklow Villa** passes Vlissingen near the end of her delivery voyage from Germany to Antwerp on 30 May 1991.*

(Ian Willett)

*The **Arklow Dew** at Garston in August 1993.*

(Stan Tedford)

M.42. **Arklow Dew** (1991 - 1994) see ship No. M.15. above.

9038397
M.43. **Arklow View** (2) (1991 -   )
O.N. 402673.   2,827g. 1,595n. 4,257d.   88,20m x 13,68m x 5,81m.
8-cyl. 4 S.C.S.A. (240mm x 330mm) MaK 8M332AK type oil engine by Krupp MaK Maschinenbau GmbH, Kiel, single reduction reverse geared to screw shaft. 1,767 bhp. 11 kts. Thwartship thrust propeller forward.

Ice-strengthened general cargo vessel, strengthened for heavy cargoes and with a 173 TEU container capacity.
105 hold/68 deck.
29.1.1991 : Keel laid by Schiffswerft Hugo Peters, Wewelsfleth, (Yard No. 638), for Invermore Shipping Ltd., Dublin.
4.8.1991 : Launched. 17.9.1991 : Completed (Arklow Shipping Ltd., managers).

M.44. **Arklow Beach**   (1991 - 1995) see ship No. A.6 in the owned fleet.

Arklow Valley (2) negotiates the 90-degree turn from the harbour entrance into the River Yare at Gorleston and prepares to head upstream to Great Yarmouth on 18 June 1995.

(Peter Pohl)

9048287
M.45. **Arklow Valley** (2) (1992 -   )
O.N. 402675.   2,827g. 1,595n. 4,254d.   88,20m x 13,68m x 5,802m.
8-cyl. 4 S.C.S.A. (240mm x 330mm) MaK 8M332AK type oil engine by Krupp MaK Maschinenbau GmbH, Kiel, single reduction reverse geared to screw shaft. 1,767 bhp. 11 kts. Thwartship thrust propeller forward.

Ice-strengthened general cargo vessel, strengthened for heavy cargoes and with a 173 TEU container capacity.
105 hold/68 deck.
21.11991 : Keel laid by Schiffswerft Hugo Peters, Wewelsfleth, (Yard No. 639), for Invermore Shipping Ltd., Dublin, (Arklow Shipping Ltd., managers). 29.8.1992 : Launched for James Tyrrell Ltd. 6.10.1992 : Completed for Invermore Shipping Ltd., Dublin, (Arklow Shipping Ltd., managers).

M.46. **Valzell** (3) (1992 - 1996) see ship No. A.10 in Arklow owned section.

*The **Valzell** (3) is seen in the West Leigh Middle Anchorage in the Thames estuary on 28 August 1991.*

(Author's collection/G. R. Wise)

6902468
M.47. **Odin**   (1992 - 1993)
O.N. 335194.   1,844g. 1,378n. 3,434d.   242' 0" x 41' 1" x 18' 9¾"
Two, 8-cyl. 4 S.C.S.A. (168mm x 184mm) DV8NM vee type oil engines by Rolls Royce Ltd., Shrewsbury, powering twin directional propellers. 1,001 bhp. 8.4 kts.

Sea-going dry-cargo barge.
1968 : Hull built by Tangen Verft AS, Kragero, (Yard No. 31). 8.1968 : Completed by Nylands Verksted, Oslo, (Yard No. 659), for Anchorage Ferrying Services Ltd, (James Fisher & Sons Ltd., Barrow in Furness, managers, later restyled James Fisher & Sons Public Limited Company). 1992 : Sold to Arklow Shipping Ltd. Arklow. 2.1993 : Sold to Friulfaktor S. R. L., Udine, Italy, (Poduzece "Luka" Rijeka, Rijeka, managers), and renamed **Mlaka**, under the Croatia flag. 12.1997 : Sold to Bin Majeed Shipping Company Ltd., Belize, and renamed **Odin**. 1.2000 : Sold to Riuby International Company Ltd., San Lorenzo. 7.2001 : Sold to unspecified owners, under the Panama flag, and renamed **Odin II**. 3.2002 : Sold to unspecified owners, under the Tonga flag. 4.2003 : Sold to unspecified owners, under the Equatorial Guinea flag, and renamed **Odin**. 2004 : Not in *Lloyd's Register,* but working in Sharjah.

*The **Odin** was built to carry phosphate rock into the dock at Whitehaven. The cargo was transhipped from geared bulk carriers anchored off the port. She was photographed at her discharging berth on 17 April 1981.*

(Bernard McCall)

7043532
M.48. **Fado** (1993)
O.N. 707310.   1,399g. 675n. 2,538d.   244' 5" x 37' 1" x 16' 4½"
Post 1975 : 1,510g. 763n. 2,538d.   80,75m x 11,33m x 5,311m.
6-cyl. 4 S.C.S.A. (320mm x 480mm) MWM TBD484-6 type oil engine by Motorenwerke Mannheim A. G. (MWM), Mannheim. 1,100 bhp. 11 kts.

Ice-strengthened general cargo vessel, strengthened for heavy cargoes.
1971 : Completed as **Diorit** by Angyalfold Shipyard, Hungarian Ship & Crane Works, Budapest, (Yard No. 2223), for KG Lübischer Seetransport GmbH & Co, Lübeck, (Otto A. Muller, Hamburg, manager). 1974 : Sold to Dolomit Hamburger Seereederei GmbH, (same manager), under the Singapore flag. 1975 : Lengthened. 1983 : Sold to Sailfast Shipping (Pte.) Ltd., Singapore, and renamed **Orchid Sea**, under the Singapore flag. 1985 : Sold to Springlight Shipping Ltd., Limassol, Cyprus, and renamed **Egbertha**. 1990 : Sold to Wateraction Shipping Ltd., Limassol, Cyprus, (MCW Bulk Chartering GmbH., Hamburg, managers), and renamed **MCW Erika**. 5.1993 : Sold to Golden Racer Shipping Ltd., Limassol, Cyprus, (Arklow Shipping Ltd., managers), and renamed **Fado**. 8.1993 : Sold to Ahmad Abdulkader Fahl, Tartous, Syria, and renamed **Ibtisam**. 1994 : Renamed **Rana M**. 1.2003 : Renamed **Amal A**. 2004 : Still in *Lloyd's Register*.

7111004
M.49. **Anseo** (1993)
O.N. 707311.   1,399g. 675n. 2,500d.   245' 6" x 37' 1" x 17' 5½"
Post 1975 : 1,510g. 763n. 2,538d.   80,75m x 11,33m x 5,311m.
6-cyl. 4 S.C.S.A. (320mm x 480mm) MWM TBD484-6 type oil engine by Motorenwerke Mannheim A. G. (MWM), Mannheim. 1,100 bhp. 11 kts.

Ice-strengthened general cargo vessel, strengthened for heavy cargoes.
1972 : Completed as **Gabbro** by Angyalfold Shipyard, Hungarian Ship & Crane Works, Budapest (Yard No. 2224), for KG Lübischer Seetransport GmbH & Co, Lübeck, (Otto A. Muller, Hamburg, manager). 1974 : Sold to Dolomit Hamburger Seereederei GmbH, (same manager), under the Singapore flag. 1975 : Lengthened. 1983 : Sold to Sailfast Shipping (Pte.) Ltd., Singapore, and renamed **Orchid Moon**. 1984 : Sold to Seatalent Navigation Ltd., Limassol, Cyprus, and renamed **Norbertha**. 1990 : Sold to Watermation Shipping Ltd., Limassol, Cyprus, (MCW Bulk Chartering GmbH, Hamburg, managers), Cyprus, and renamed **MCW Ilsabe**. 5.1993 : Sold to Golden Racer Shipping Ltd., Limassol, Cyprus, (Arklow Shipping Ltd., managers), and renamed **Anseo**. 8.1993 : Sold to Ahmad Abdulkader Fahl, Tartous, Syria, and renamed **Nawal**. 2004 : Still in *Lloyd's Register*.

*The **Fado** and **Anseo** were photographed at the Parkkade, Rotterdam, on 2 June 1993. Their Gaelic names are translated into English as "long ago" and "here" respectively.*

(Bernard McCall)

7127235
M. 50. **Anois** (1993)
O.N. 707312.   1,399g. 675n. 2,538d.   244' 5" x 37' 1" x 16' 4½"
Post 1975 : 1,510g. 763n. 2,445d.   80,68m x 11,33m x 5,311m.
6-cyl. 4 S.C.S.A. (320mm x 480mm) MWM TBD484-6 type oil engine by Motorenwerke Mannheim A. G. (MWM),
Mannheim. 1,100 bhp. 11 kts.

Ice-strengthened general cargo vessel, strengthened for heavy cargoes.
1971 : Completed as **Granit** by Angyalfold Shipyard, Hungarian Ship & Crane Works, Budapest (Yard No. 2225), for KG
Lübischer Seetransport GmbH & Co, Lübeck, (Otto A. Muller, Hamburg, manager). 1972 : Sold to Dolomit Hamburger
Seereederei GmbH, (same manager), under the Singapore flag. 1975 : Lengthened. 1983 : Sold to Sailfast Shipping
(Pte.) Ltd., Singapore, and renamed **Orchid Sun**. 1984 : Sold to Springlight Shipping Ltd., Limassol, Cyprus, and renamed
Hermana. 1990 : Sold to Watergalaxy Shipping Ltd., Limassol, Cyprus, (MCW Bulk Chartering GmbH, Hamburg,
managers), Cyprus, and renamed **MCW Rita**. 5.1993 : Sold to Golden Racer Shipping Ltd., Limassol, Cyprus, (Arklow
Shipping Ltd., managers), and renamed **Anois**. 8.1993 : Sold to Wahib Kamel Marai & Tarek Abdulrahman Byized, (Al
Wahib Import & Export, managers), Tartous, Syria, and renamed **Wahib M**. 2004 : Still in *Lloyd's Register*.

The **Anois** was photographed at Rotterdam in June 1993. Her Gaelic name translates into English as "now".
(Author's collection/R. Zwama)

The **Arklow Brook** (2) arrives at Tilbury Grain Terminal on 31 August 2002 at the end of a voyage from Bordeaux. She departed for Amsterdam five days later.

(Dominic McCall)

9101534
M.51. **Arklow Brook** (2)   (1995 -   )
O.N. 402873.   4,783g. 2,519n. 7,184d.   99,95m x 17,06m x 6,764m.
6-cyl. 4 S.C.S.A. (320mm x 480mm) MaK 6M32 type oil engine by Krupp MaK Maschinenbau GmbH, Kiel, single reduction reverse geared to screw shaft with controllable pitch propeller. 3,589 bhp. 12 kts. Thwartship thrust propeller forward.

19.9.1994 : Keel laid by Appledore Shipbuilders Ltd., Appledore, (Yard No. 160), for Devon Line, Dorchester, (Arklow Shipping Ltd., managers), Arklow. 1.7.1995 : Launched. 29.8.1995 : Completed.

*The **Arklow Spirit** makes cautious progress in the River Neath having just left Giants Wharf at Briton Ferry on the evening of 16 April 2003. Her cargo was steel coils.*

(Bill Moore)

9117959
M.52. **Arklow Spirit**   (1995 - 1998)
O.N. 402872.   2,271g. 1,290n. 3,211d.   89,95m x 12,71m x 4,652m.
8-cyl. 4 S.C.S.A. (200mm x 300mm) MaK 8M20 type oil engine by Krupp MaK Maschinenbau GmbH, Kiel, single reduction reverse geared to screw shaft with fixed pitch propeller. 1,849 bhp. 10.5 kts. Thwartship thrust propeller forward.

General cargo vessel strengthened for heavy cargoes with a 116 TEU container capacity. 76 hold/40 deck.
12.1.1995 : Keel laid by Schps. & Mfbk Barkmeijer Stroobos B. V., Stroobos, (Yard No. 278), for James Tyrrell, (Arklow Shipping Ltd., managers), Arklow. 16.6.1995 : Launched. 8.7.1995 : Completed. 1998 : Sold to Arklow Shipping Ltd.

M.53. **Dunkerque Express**   (1995 - 1999) see ship No. M.24 above.

9101546
M.54. **Arklow Bridge** (3)   (1995 -   )
O.N. 402874.   4,783g. 2,519n. 7,184d.   99,95m x 17,06m x 6,764m.
6-cyl. 4 S.C.S.A. (320mm x 480mm) MaK 6M32 type oil engine by Krupp MaK Maschinenbau GmbH, Kiel, single reduction reverse geared to screw shaft with controllable pitch propeller. 3,589 bhp. 12.5 kts. Thwartship thrust propeller forward.

17.5.1995 : Keel laid by Appledore Shipbuilders Ltd., Appledore, (Yard No. 161), for Arklow Shipping Ltd. 4.11.1995 : Launched for Devon Line, Dorchester, (Arklow Shipping Ltd., managers), Arklow. 3.1.1996 : Completed.

The **Dunkerque Express** at Rotterdam's Parkkade on 20 May 1995. She had been renamed from **Inisheer** in early March of that year and was linking Europoort to Dunkerque and Antwerp with occasional calls at Felixstowe.

(Jim McFaul)

The **Arklow Bridge** (3) is seen at Terneuzen.

(Ron Wood)

9117961

M.55. **Arklow Spray** (1996 - 1998)

O.N. 402875.   2,300g. 1,290n. 3,193d.   89,95m x 12,71m x 4,64m.

8-cyl. 4 S.C.S.A. (200mm x 300mm) MaK 8M20 type oil engine by Krupp MaK Maschinenbau GmbH, Kiel, single reduction reverse geared to screw shaft with fixed pitch propeller. 1,849 bhp.   10.5 kts. Thwartship thrust propeller forward.

General cargo vessel strengthened for heavy cargoes with a 116 TEU container capacity. 76 hold/40 deck.

3.6.1995 : Keel laid by Schps. & Mfbk Barkmeijer Stroobos B. V., Stroobos, (Yard No. 279), for James Tyrrell, (Arklow Shipping Ltd., managers), Arklow. 17.11.1995 : Launched. 28.1.1996 : Completed. 1998 : Sold to Arklow Shipping Ltd.

The **Arklow Spray** was photographed in The Wash on 26 July 2003. She was heading for the Lincolnshire port of Boston where she loaded a cargo of grain.

(David Dixon)

Battery Point at Portishead is a popular vantage point for watching ships heading to or from Sharpness, Portbury and Avonmouth. In recent years, the **Arklow Castle** has maintained a successful weekly service linking Avonmouth to Bilbao with calls at Greenock and Dublin on her outward voyage. She usually arrives in Avonmouth on a Sunday or Monday and we see her here inward bound to Avonmouth on 1 September 2002.

(Bernard McCall)

9141106

M.56. **Arklow Castle** (2)   (1996 -   )

O.N. 402876.   5,006g.   2,096n.   6,807d.   116,40m (BB) x 19,50m x 7,06m

9-cyl. 4 S.C.S.A. (320mm x 480mm) MaK 9M32 type oil engine by Krupp MaK Maschinenbau GmbH, Kiel, single reduction reverse geared to screw shaft with controllable pitch propeller. 5,384 bhp. 16.5 kts. Thwartship thrust controllable pitch propeller forward.

Fixed-guide containership with a 532 TEU capacity. 134 hold/398 deck (inc. 40 refrigerated).

5.12.1995 : Keel laid by Schiffswerft Hugo Peters, Wewelsfleth, (Yard No. 657), for Arklow Shipping Ltd.   10.8.1996 : Launched for Arklow Containers Ltd., (Arklow Shipping Ltd., managers), Arklow.   3.10.1996 : Completed.

8815293

M.57. **Inishowen** (2)   (1996 - 1998)

O.N. 402878.   2,749g.   1,110n.   3,146d.   94,50m (BB) x 16,14m x 5,005m.

6-cyl. 4 S.C.S.A. (320mm x 350mm) Wärtsilä 6R32D type oil engine by Oy Wärtsilä Ab, Turku/Åbo, Finland, geared to a controllable pitch propeller. 1,353 bhp. 14.5 kts. Thwartship thrust propeller forward.

Ice-strengthened general cargo vessel strengthened for heavy cargoes and with a 262 TEU container capacity. 82 hold/180 deck.

9.9.1988 : Keel laid as **Angela Jurgens** by J. J. Sietas GmbH & Co KG Schiffsw. Hamburg, (Yard No. 967), for KG Schiffahrtsgesellschaft Klaus Jurgens m.s. Angela Jurgens GmbH & Co, Hamburg. 19.10.1988 : Launched.   11.12.1988 : Completed.   1996 : Purchased by Coastal Shipping PLC, Arklow, (Arklow Shipping Ltd., managers), and renamed **Inishowen**. 1998 : Sold to Scheepvaartonderneming Gera C. V., Heerenveen, (Holwerda Shipmanagement B.V., Heerenveen, managers), and renamed **Gera**, under the Netherlands flag. 2001 : Renamed **Arfell**.

Inishowen (2) at Dublin on 16 February 1998, with mainmast lowered.

(Author's collection / T. O'Connalain)

8121379
M.58. *Inishfree* (2) (1997 - 2000)
O.N. 402877. 3,222g. 1,743n. 5,412d. 82,38m (BB) x 15,83m x 7,46m.
6-cyl. 4 S.C.S.A. (320mm x 350mm) Wärtsilä 6R32 type oil engine by Oy Wärtsilä Ab, Turku/Åbo, Finland, geared to a controllable pitch propeller. 2,780 bhp. 11.5kts. Thwartship thrust propeller forward.

Ice-strengthened general cargo vessel with a 146 TEU container capacity.
26.10.1982 : Keel laid as *Lenneborg* by Nieuwe Noord Nederlandse Scheepswerven B.V., Groningen, (Yard No. 404), for Linde Lloyd Zeeschepen III B.V., Rotterdam, (Wagenborg Shipping B.V., managers), Delfzijl, Netherlands. 23.4.1983 : Launched. 20.5.1983 : Completed. 1997 : Purchased by Coastal Shipping PLC, (Arklow Shipping Ltd., managers), and renamed *Inishfree* . 21.2.1997 : Whilst berthed at Newport, Gwent, suffered a galley fire resulting in the loss of 1 life and 3 other injuries. 4.2000 : Sold to Anral Lines Ltd., Guyana, (Anral Investments Ltd., Guyana, managers), and renamed *Sabina A*, under the St. Vincent & the Grenadines flag. 13.5.2002 : Ocean Management Inc, Georgetown, Guyana. appointed as managers.

The *Inishfree* (2) is seen at the North Quay adjacent to her owners' offices in her home port of Arklow on 28 October 1997. She was undergoing maintenance and minor modifications at the time.

(Pat Davis)

8914295
M.59. *Arklow Fortune* (1997 -   )
O.N. 402880. 2,373g. 1,434n. 4,250d. 88,25m (BB) x 13,21m x 5,45m.
6-cyl. 4 S.C.S.A. (280mm x 300mm) Caterpillar 3606TA type oil engine by Caterpillar Inc, Peoria, Illinois, geared to a controllable pitch propeller. 2,175 bhp. 12 kts. Thwartship thrust propeller forward.

Ice-strengthened general cargo vessel with a 96 TEU container capacity.
18.3.1991 : Keel laid as *MB Humber* by B. V. Scheepswerf "Ferus Smit" Foxhol, (Yard No. 283), for Sprante Schiffahrts-Verwaltungs GmbH, Brunsbüttel, Germany. 14.7.1991 : Launched. Intended for the Antigua and Barbuda flag. 4.12.1991 : Completed for C. F. Ahrenkiel (I. O. M.) Ltd., Castletown, Isle of Man, (C. F. Ahrenkiel Shipmanagement [Cyprus] Ltd, Limassol, managers), under the Liberia flag. 1997 : Purchased by Amoy Enterprises Ltd., Arklow, (Arklow Shipping Ltd., managers) and renamed *Arklow Fortune*. 2.2004 : Sold to Invermore Shipping Ltd., Dublin, (same managers).

When first taken over, the **Arklow Fortune** and her three sisterships retained the dark green hull colour of their previous owner. The **Arklow Fortune** approaches Eastham Locks on 24 June 1997 on her first visit to the Manchester Ship Canal as an Arklow vessel.
(Ambuscade Marine Photography)

*In her more familiar Arklow livery, the **Arklow Fortune** passes Battery Point at Portishead on her way down the Bristol Channel on 1 November 2003.*

(Bernard McCall)

8922254
M.60. **Arklow Fame** (1997 -   )
O.N. 402881.   2,373g. 1,434n. 4,220d.   88,25m (BB) x 13,21m x 5,463m.
6-cyl. 4 S.C.S.A. (280mm x 300mm) Caterpillar 3606TA type oil engine by Caterpillar Inc, Peoria, Illinois, geared to a controllable pitch propeller. 2,175 bhp. 12 kts. Thwartship thrust propeller forward.

Ice-strengthened general cargo vessel with a 96 TEU container capacity.
18.3.1992 : Keel laid as **MB Avon** by Ferus Smit Hoogezand B.V., Hoogezand, (Yard No. 285) for Sprante Schiffahrts-Verwaltungs GmbH, Brunsbüttel, Germany. 17.6.1992 : Launched. Intended for Antigua and Barbuda flag. 31.7 1992 : Completed for C. F. Ahrenkiel (I. O. M.) Ltd., Castletown, Isle of Man, (C. F. Ahrenkiel Shipmanagement (Cyprus) Ltd, Limassol, managers), under the Liberia flag. 1997 : Purchased by Ross Quay Ltd., Arklow, (Arklow Shipping Ltd., managers) and renamed **Arklow Fame**. 2.2004 : Sold to Invermore Shipping Ltd., Dublin, (same managers).

*Sadly the weather did not live up to the occasion for it was a rather overcast day when the **Arklow Fame** was being renamed. The location is Dublin and the date is 1 July 1997. Again, the ship retains the hull and upperworks colours of her previous owners at this time.*

(Author's collection/T. O'Connalain)

The **Arklow Fame** approaches Liverpool Docks on 21 June 1998 at the end of a voyage from Santander. She left two days later, bound for Bilbao with a cargo of scrap.

(David Williams)

The **Arklow Freedom** seen outward bound from Belfast.

(Author's collection/Alan Geddes)

8914283
M.61. **Arklow Freedom** (1997 -   )
O.N. 402879.   2,373g. 1,434n. 4,250d.   88,25(BB) x 13,21m x 5,463m.
6-cyl. 4 S.C.S.A. (280mm x 300mm) Caterpillar 3606TA type oil engine by Caterpillar Inc, Peoria, Illinois, geared to a controllable pitch propeller. 2,175 bhp. 12 kts. Thwartship thrust propeller forward.

Ice-strengthened general cargo vessel with a 96 TEU container capacity.
18.3.1991: Keel laid as **MB Clyde** by B. V. Scheepswerf "Ferus Smit", Foxhol, (Yard No. 284), for Sprante Schiffahrts-Verwaltungs GmbH, Brunsbuttel, Germany. 20.3.1992 : Launched. Intended for Antigua and Barbuda flag. 8.5.1992 : Completed for C. F. Ahrenkiel (I. O. M.) Ltd., Castletown, Isle of Man, (C. F. Ahrenkiel Shipmanagement (Cyprus) Ltd, Limassol, managers), under the Liberia flag. 1997 : Purchased by Amoy Enterprises Ltd., Arklow, (Arklow Shipping Ltd., managers), and renamed **Arklow Freedom**. 2.2004 : Sold to Invermore Shipping Ltd., Dublin, (same managers).

8922266

M.62. **Arklow Faith** (1997 -   )
O.N. 402882.   2,373g. 1,434n. 4,220d.   88,25m (BB) x 13,21m x 5,45m.
6-cyl. 4 S.C.S.A. (280mm x 300mm) Caterpillar 3606TA type oil engine by Caterpillar Inc, Peoria, Illinois, geared to a controllable pitch propeller. 2,175 bhp. 12 kts. Thwartship thrust propeller forward.

Ice-strengthened general cargo vessel with a 96 TEU container capacity.
10.3.1992 : Keel laid as **MB Thames** by Ferus Smit Hoogezand B.V., Hoogezand, (Yard No. 286) for Sprante Schiffahrts-Verwaltungs GmbH. Brunsbuttel, Germany. 24.10.1992 : Launched for C. F. Ahrenkiel (I. O. M.) Ltd., Castletown, Isle of Man, (C. F. Ahrenkiel Shipmanagement (Cyprus) Ltd, Limassol, managers). 24.12.1992 : Completed, under the Liberia flag. 1997 : Purchased by Coastal Partnership (1997) Ltd., Arklow, (Arklow Shipping Ltd., managers) and renamed **Arklow Faith**. 29.4.2000 : Whilst on a voyage from Runcorn to Wilhelmshaven suffered main engine failure in a position 50. 36N., 06.02W. 30.4.2000 : Taken in tow bound to Falmouth for repairs, and returned to service in early May.

In the view on the left, dated 24 July 2001, the **Arklow Faith** *gets underway from Latchford Locks on the Manchester Ship Canal, heading for Cerestar Wharf in Manchester with a cargo of maize. In the lower photograph, the same vessel still has cream upperworks as she approaches Imperial Wharf, Gravesend, on 28 January 1998.*

(Dominic McCall, left; Kevin Bassett, lower)

*These photographs provide a good insight into one method of construction favoured by Dutch shipyards. The ships are built in sections, not always at the same location, and these sections are then assembled. The **Arklow Sand** still awaited the fitting of a bow section at the Barkmeijer shipyard in Stroobos when she was photographed on 20 September 1997.*

(Martin Penwright)

*It would be a further two months following this photograph before the **Arklow Star** was launched. She was photographed at the Barkmeijer slipway on 14 May 1999.*

(Stan Tedford)

9163611
M.63. *Arklow Sand* (1998 - 2002)
O.N. 19109.   2,316g. 1,295n. 3,193d.   89,98m x 12,71m x 4,652 m.
8-cyl. 4 S.C.S.A. (200mm x 300mm) MaK 8M20 type oil engine by MaK Motoren GmbH & Co KG, Kiel, single reduction reverse geared to screw shaft with fixed pitch propeller. 2,066 bhp. 11.5 kts. Thwartship thrust propeller forward.

General cargo vessel, strengthened for heavy cargoes and with a 116 TEU container caacity. 76 hold/40 deck.
3.4.1997 : Keel laid by Schps. & Mfbk Barkmeijer Stroobos B. V., Stroobos, (Yard No. 281), for Arklow Shipping Ltd.
11.12.1997 : Launched. 9.1.1998 : Completed for Arklow Shipping Ltd., (Arklow Shipping Ltd., Arklow, managers), under the Netherlands flag. 1998 : Transferred to Rederij Sonnega B. V., Rotterdam, (same managers). 2002 : Arklow Shipping Nederland B.V., Rotterdam, appointed as managers.

The roofs of the buildings in Aberdeen still have a light covering of snow and there is a hint of ice on the water but it was a sunny 19 January 1998 when the **Arklow Sand** *visited the port. She had been completed only ten days previously and was still considered to be on trials at the time.*

(Bill Newlands)

Saturday, 25 October 1998 was a notable date in Arklow's maritime history. On this date, the **Arklow Sea** became the first Dutch-registered Arklow ship to visit her "home" port. Furthermore, she loaded the port's biggest-ever export cargo, namely 3000 tonnes of fertiliser.

(Pat Davis)

9163623
M.64. *Arklow Sea* (1998 - 2002)
O.N. 19159.   2,316g. 1,295n. 3,193d.   89,98m x 12,71m x 4,652m.
8-cyl. 4 S.C.S.A. (200mm x 300mm) MaK 8M20 type oil engine by MaK Motoren GmbH & Co KG, Kiel, single reduction reverse geared to screw shaft with fixed pitch propeller. 2,066 bhp. 11.5 kts. Thwartship thrust propeller forward.

General cargo vessel strengthened for heavy cargoes and with a 116 TEU container capacity. 76 hold/40 deck.
6.10.1997 : Keel laid by Schps. & Mfbk Barkmeijer Stroobos B. V., Stroobos, (Yard No. 286), for Arklow Shipping Ltd.
7.3.1998 : Launched for Arklow Shipping B.V., Rotterdam, (Arklow Shipping Ltd., Arklow, managers).   14.3.1998 : Completed for Rederij Makkinga B. V., (same managers), under the Netherlands flag. 2002 : Arklow Shipping Nederland B.V., Rotterdam, appointed as managers.

9196254
M.65. *Arklow Star* (1999 - 2002)
O.N. 19486.   2,316g. 1,295n. 3,193d.   89,98m x 12,71m x 4,652m.
8-cyl. 4 S.C.S.A. (200mm x 300mm) MaK 8M20 type oil engine by MaK Motoren GmbH & Co KG, Kiel, single reduction reverse geared to screw shaft with fixed pitch propeller. 2,066 bhp. 11.5 kts. Thwartship thrust propeller forward.

General cargo vessel strengthened for heavy cargoes and with a 154 TEU container capacity. 114 hold/40 deck.
29.6.1998 : Keel laid by Schps. & Mfbk Barkmeijer Stroobos B. V., Stroobos, (Yard No. 290), for Arklow Shipping B. V., Rotterdam, (Arklow Shipping Ltd., managers).   23.7.1999 : Launched.   10.9.1999 : Completed for Rederij Steggerda B. V., Rotterdam, (same managers). 2002 : Arklow Shipping Nederland B.V., Rotterdam, appointed as managers.

Medina Wharf on the west bank of the River Medina in Cowes, Isle of Wight, is the setting for the **Arklow Star** *on 24 April 2000.*

(Brian Ralfs)

The **Arklow Dawn** *(2) still had two deck cranes when seen in the New Waterway outward bound from Rotterdam on 18 May 2001.More photographs of this ship are on pages 90/91.*

(Reinier van der Wetering)

8116984

M.66. **Arklow Dawn** (2)   (1999 - 2003)
O.N. 402888   7,944g. 5,104n. 12,078d.   129,04m x 20,05m x 8,419m.
Post 1994 : 8,353g. 4,305n. 12,296d.
Post 1995 : 8,353g. 4,305n. 12,271d.
9-cyl. 4 S.C.S.A. (400mm x 460mm) Pielstick 9PC2-5L-400 type oil engine by Nippon Kokan K. K., Yokohama. 5,850 bhp.
13.5 kts.

12.11.1982 : Launched as **Falknes** by Miho Zosensho K. K., Shimizu, Shizouka Pref., (Yard No. 1211) for PR Falknes, (AS Kristian Jebsen Rederi, Bergen, managers), Norway. 24.2.1983 : Completed. 1986 : Transferred to Emporium Shipping Corp., Manila, (same managers), and renamed **General Fitnes** * then **Fitnes**, (O.N. 228976), under the Philippines flag. 1987 : AS Jebsens Ship Management (JSMA), Bergen, appointed as managers. 1988 : Renamed **Falknes**. 1989 : Jebsen Ship Management (Bergen) AS appointed as managers. 1990 : Transferred to Panama flag (Chelston Ship Management Ltd., managers) (O.N. 17095-87B). 1991 : Jebsens Ship Management (Bergen) AS appointed as managers. 1993 : Sold to Massoel S. A., Geneva, and renamed **Uri**. 1993 : Acomarit Services Maritimes S. A., Geneva, appointed managers, and transferred to the Switzerland flag. 1996 : Sold to Masstransport M. T. S. A., Fribourg, (same managers). 1997 : Sold to Golden Fair Shipping S. A., Panama, (Harbor Fair Development Ltd., managers), and renamed **Daisy Green**. 1999/2000 : Purchased at a Rotterdam auction by Coastal Shipping Ltd., (Arklow Shipping Ltd., managers), and renamed **Arklow Dawn**, retaining Panama flag. 2000 : Transferred to Irish flag. 10.2000 : Dry-docked at Dublin for first overhaul since purchase. 16.12.2003 : Sold to Polydefkis Maritime Ltd., Piraeus, (Sea Observer Shipping Ltd., Limassol, managers), Greece, and renamed **Polydefkis** under the Malta Flag. 2004 : Still in *Lloyd's Register*.

* Although the name **General Fitnes** appears on some official documents, it seems that it was never intended to be an official renaming; rather it was human error which added the word "General" at a time when other vessels in the fleet were being renamed with this prefix.

M.67. **Inisheer**   (1999 - 2002) see ship No. M.24 above.

8116960
M.68. **Diane Green** / **Arklow Day** (2) (2000 - 2003)
O.N. 402889   7,367g. 4,995n. 12,334d.   129,04m x 20,05m x 8,419m.
Post 1994 : 8,351g. 4,305n. 12,296d.
Post 1995 : 8,351g. 4,305n. 12,334d.
9-cyl. 4 S.C.S.A. (400mm x 460mm) Pielstick 9PC2-5L-400 type oil engine by Nippon Kokan K. K., Yokohama. 5,850 bhp.
13.75 kts.

26.4.1982 : Launched as **Fjellnes** by Miho Zosensho K. K., Shimizu, Shizouka Pref., (Yard No. 1209), for AS Kristian Jebsen Rederi, Bergen. 5.8.1982 : Completed for Sangrail Companhia Naviera S. A., Panama, (AS Kristian Jebsen Rederi, Bergen, managers), under the Panama flag. 1985 : Transferred to Jebsens Fjellnes Shipping S. A., Panama, (same managers). 1986 : Transferred to Philippines flag, and renamed **Fastnes**, (AS Jebsen Ship Management (JSMA), Bergen, managers). 1989 : Jebsen Ship Management (Bergen) AS, Bergen, appointed as managers. 1990 : Chelston Ship Management Ltd., London, appointed as managers. 1992 : Transferred to Panama flag, Jebsens Ship Management (Bergen) AS, Bergen, appointed as managers). 1993 : Sold to Massoel S. A., Fribourg, Switzerland, and renamed **Sarine 2**. 1994 : Acomarit Services Maritimes S. A., Geneva, appointed as managers and transferred to the Switzerland flag. 1996 : Sold to Harbor Fair Shipping S. A., Panama, (Perpetual Shipmanagement International Inc., managers), and renamed **Diane Green**. 1997 : Harbor Fair Development Ltd. appointed as managers. 3.2000 : Purchased at an auction in Trinidad, via their bankers by Arklow Shipping Ltd. 7.2000 : Dry-docked for overhaul at Dublin, transferred to Coastal Shipping PLC, Arklow, (Arklow Shipping Ltd., managers), Arklow, and renamed **Arklow Day**. (O.N. 402889). 6.11.2003 : Sold to Castor Maritime, Piraeus, (Sea Observer Shipping, managers), and renamed **Castor** under the Malta Flag. 2004 : Still in *Lloyd's Register*.

The **Arklow Day** (2) is seen at Blyth on 6 June 2003. She and the other D class ships were trading regularly between Blyth and Aughinish at this time.

(Iain McCall)

73

8701947
M.69. **Arklow Dusk** (2000 - 2004)
O.N. 402890. 8,907g. 4,307n. 11,722d.   143,70m x   x 8,30m.
6-cyl. 2 S.C.S.A. (500mm x 1620mm) B&W 6L50MCE type engine by H. Cegielski Zaklady Przemyslu Metalowego. Poznan. 5,182 bhp. 13.5 kts.

10.8.1990 : Keel laid as **Kopalnia Ziemowit** by Stocznia Szczecinska im A. Warskiego, Szczecin, (Yard No. 547/04) for the Polish Shipping Company (Zegluga Polska Spolka Akcyjna), Poland. 21.12.1990 : Launched. 24.10.1991 : Completed. 7.2000 : Purchased by Coastal Shipping PLC (Arklow Shipping Ltd., managers), Arklow, and renamed **Arklow Dusk**. 2004 : Sold to Adinus Transportes, Switzerland, (Navimar S.A., Lugano, managers), and renamed **Rubicone**, retaining Irish flag.

The **Arklow Dusk** at Southampton on 15 June 2002. She had arrived three days earlier from Tarragona.

(Bernard McCall)

9218222
M.70. **Arklow Surf** (2000 - 2001)
2,316g. 1,295n. 3,193d.   89,98m x 12,64m x 4,652m.
8-cyl. 4 S.C.S.A. (200mm x 300mm) MaK 8M20 type oil engine by MaK Motoren GmbH & Company K.G., Kiel, single reduction reverse geared to screw shaft with controllable pitch propeller. 2,066 bhp. 11kts. Thwartship thrust propeller forward.

General cargo vessel strengthened for heavy cargoes and with a 154 TEU container capacity. 114 hold/40 deck.
30.6.1998 : Keel laid by Schps. & Mfbk Barkmeijer Stroobos B. V., Stroobos, (Yard No. 294), for Arklow Shipping Ltd. 20.10.2000 : Launched for Scheepvaartmaatschappij Hunzeland C.V., Rotterdam, Netherlands, (Arklow Shipping Ltd., managers. 6.11.2000 : Completed. 2001 : Arklow Shipping Nederland B.V., Rotterdam, appointed as managers.

Having arrived from Belfast, the **Arklow Surf** loads barley in Aberdeen on 7 March 2004.

(David Dodds)

9238404
M.71. **Arklow River** (4)   (2002 -   )
O.N. 403334.   2,999g. 1,635n. 4,530d.   89,99m x 14,18m x 5,68m.
6-cyl. 4 S.C.S.A. (255mm x 400mm) MaK 6M25 type oil engine by Caterpillar Motoren GmbH & Co KG, Kiel, single reduction reverse geared to screw shaft with controllable pitch propeller. 2,038 bhp. 11.5 kts. Thwartship thrust propeller forward.

Multi-purpose cargo vessel with 74 TEU container capacity. 38 hold/36 deck.
2000 : Ordered from Schps. & Mfbk Barkmeijer Stroobos B. V., Stroobos, (Yard No. 300), for associates of Arklow Shipping Ltd., (Arklow Shipping Ltd., managers). 5.1.2002 : Keel laid. 17.1.2003 : Launched. 27.2.2003 : Completed.

The **Arklow River** (4) fully laden in the River Mersey.

(Darren B Hillman)

9287314
M.72. **Arklow Wind**   (2004 -   )
O.N. 403338.   8,938g. 4,815n 13,777d.   136,4m (BB) x 21,25m x 8,35m.
6-cyl. 4 S.C.S.A. (380mm x 475mm) Wärtsilä 6L38B type oil engine by Wärtsilä-Finland Oy, Finland, reduction geared to controllable pitch propeller. 5,438 bhp. 13.5 kts. Bow thrust unit forward.

12.8.2003 : Keel laid by Kyokuyo Zosen K. K., Shimoneseki / Chofu (Yard No. 448), for Coastal Shipping Ltd., Arklow, (Arklow Shipping Ltd., managers). 5.10.2003 : Launched. 15.1.2004 : Completed.

9291705
M.73. **Arklow Rock**   (2004 -   )
2,999g. 1,635n. 4,530d.   89,99m x 14,18m x 5,68m
6-cyl. 4 S.C.S.A. (255mm x 400mm) MaK 6M25 type oil engine by Caterpillar Motoren GmbH & Co KG, Kiel, single reduction reverse geared to screw shaft with controllable pitch propeller. 2,038 bhp. 11.5 kts. Thwartship thrust propeller forward.

Multi-purpose cargo vessel with 74 TEU container capacity. 38 hold/36 deck.
10.9.2003 : Keel laid by Schps. & Mfbk Barkmeijer Stroobos B. V., Stroobos, (Yard No. 303), for associates of Arklow Shipping Ltd., (Arklow Shipping Ltd., managers). 27.2.2004 : Launched. 11.4.2004 : Completed.

9291717
M.74. **Arklow Rover** (2004 -   )
2,999g. 1,635n. 4,530d. 89,99m x 14,18m x 5,68m.
6-cyl. 4 S.C.S.A. (255mm x 400mm) MaK 6M25 type oil engine by Caterpillar Motoren GmbH & Co KG, Kiel, single reduction reverse geared to screw shaft with controllable pitch propeller. 2,038 bhp. 11.5 kts. Thwartship thrust propeller forward.

Multi-purpose cargo-vessel with 74 TEU container capacity. 38 hold/36 deck.
11.11.2003 : Keel laid by Schps. & Mfbk Barkmeijer Stroobos B. V., Stroobos, (Yard No. 304), for associates of Arklow Shipping Ltd., (Arklow Shipping Ltd., managers). 4.5.2004 : Launched. 15.7.2004 : Completed.

9201839
M.75. **Arklow Venture** (2) (2004 -   )
2,829g 1,548n, 4996d 89,75m x 13,60m x 6,36m
6-cyl. 4 S.C.S.A. (255mm x 400mm) MaK oil engine by MaK Motoren GmbH & Co KG, Kiel, geared to controllable pitch propeller. 2,447bhp. 12.2 kts.

21.7.1999 : Launched by Scheepswerf Pattje B. V., Waterhuizen,(Yard No. 409), as **Sider Venture** for Albar Holdings Inc., (Italtech S.r.l., Naples, managers); Portugal (Madeira) flag. 13.10.1999 : Handed over at Delfzijl. 9.2004 : acquired by Invermore Shipping Ltd., Arklow, (Arklow Shipping Ltd., Arklow, managers); handed over in Naples and renamed **Arklow Venture** under the Ireland flag.

Vessels Under Construction

9314600
Arklow Willow (2004 -   )
8,938g. 4,815n 13,988d. 136,4m (BB) x 21,25m x 8,35m.
6-cyl. S.C.S.A. (380mm x 475mm) Wärtsilä 6L38B type oil engine by Wärtsilä-Finland Oy, Finland, reduction geared to controllable pitch propeller. 5,438bhp. 13.5 kts. Bow thrust unit forward.

1.2004 : Optional Contract by Kyokuyo Zosen K. K., Shimoneseki / Chofu, (Yard No. 460), taken up by Arklow Shipping Ltd.

9291729
Arklow Rainbow / Arklow Racer (2004 -   )
2,999g. 1,635n. 4,530d. 89,99m x 14,18m x 5,68m.
6-cyl. 4 S.C.S.A. (255mm x 400mm) MaK 6M25 type oil engine by Caterpillar Motoren GmbH & Co KG, Kiel, single reduction reverse geared to screw shaft with controllable pitch propeller. 2,038 bhp. 11.5 kts. Thwartship thrust propeller forward.

Multi-purpose cargo vessel with 74 TEU container capacity. 38 hold/36 deck.
2003 : Ordered from Schps. & Mfbk Barkmeijer Stroobos B. V., Stroobos, (Yard No. 305), for associates of Arklow Shipping Ltd., (Arklow Shipping Ltd., managers). 24.3.2004 : Keel laid as **Arklow Rainbow**. 2004 : Launched as **Arklow Racer**.

9291731
Arklow Rebel (2005 -   )
2,999g. 1,635n. 4,530d. 89,99m x 14,18m x 5,68m.
6-cyl. 4 S.C.S.A. (255mm x 400mm) MaK 6M25 type oil engine by Caterpillar Motoren GmbH & Co KG, Kiel, single reduction reverse geared to screw shaft with controllable pitch propeller. 2,038 bhp. 11.5 kts. Thwartship thrust propeller forward.

Multi-purpose cargo vessel with 74 TEU container capacity. 38 hold/36 deck.
2003 : Ordered from Schps. & Mfbk Barkmeijer Stroobos B. V., Stroobos, (Yard No. 306), for associates of Arklow Shipping Ltd., (Arklow Shipping Ltd., managers).

Cross River Ferries Ltd

Cork

Owned 50% with Marine Transport Services Ltd.

7028386
CRF.1. **Carrigaloe** (1995 -   ) twin screw ferry.
O.N. 402808.   225g. 101n. 96d.   161' 5" x 42' 5" x 4' 1"
Two, 8-cyl. 4 S. C. S. A. (140mm x 197mm) engines by L. Gardner & Sons Ltd., Manchester, geared to a directional propeller forward and aft. 460 bhp. 8 kts.

200 deck passenger, RoRo deck cargo ferry / bow and stern door-ramps.
11.1.1970 : Keel laid as **Kyleakin** by Newport Shipbuilding and Engineering Ltd., Newport, (Yard No. 99) for the Caledonian Steam Packet Company Ltd., Glasgow. 24.7.1970 : Launched. 1.8.1970 : Completed. 1973 : Owners restyled as Caledonian McBrayne Ltd., (David McBrayne Ltd., managers). 1985 : Removed from management. 1992 : Sold to Cross River Ferries Ltd., Cobh, Republic of Ireland, and renamed **Carrigaloe**. 1995 : Clyde Shipping Company's 50% shareholding sold to Arklow Shipping Ltd., Arklow. 2002 : Chartered out to Lough Foyle Ferry Company Ltd., Greencastle, for a new service across the mouth of Lough Foyle (Greencastle, County Donegal, Republic of Ireland – Magilligan Point, County Londonderry, Northern Ireland). 2003 : Returned to service at Cobh.

The **Carrigaloe** approaches Glenbrook, near Passage West, from Carrigaloe, near Cobh on Great Island, on a wet summer day in August 2000. She entered service on the route in March 1993. The crossing takes four minutes.

(Bernard McCall)

7101607
CRF.2. **Glenbrook** (1995 -   ) twin screw ferry.
O.N. 402812.   225g. 101n. 79d.   161' 5" x 42' 5" x 4' 1"
Two, 8-cyl. 4 S. C. S. A. (140mm x 197mm) engines by L. Gardner & Sons Ltd., Manchester, geared to a directional propeller forward and aft. 460 bhp. 8 kts.

200 deck passenger, RoRo deck cargo ferry / bow and stern door-ramps.
3.8.1970 : Keel laid as **Lochalsh** by Newport Shipbuilding and Engineering Ltd., Newport, (Yard No. 100) for the Caledonian Steam Packet Company Ltd., Glasgow. 12.2.1971 : Launched. 17.3.1971 : Completed. 1973 : Owners restyled as Caledonian McBrayne Ltd., (David McBrayne Ltd., managers). 1985 : Removed from management. 1993 : Sold to Cross River Ferries Ltd., Cobh, Republic of Ireland, and renamed **Glenbrook**. 1995 : Clyde Shipping Company's 50% shareholding sold to Arklow Shipping Ltd., Arklow.

*Seen at a similar vantage point to the previous photograph, the **Glenbrook** was operating the crossing between the village after which she is named and Carrigaloe on 28 May 2003.*

(Dominic McCall)

Coastal Shipping Ltd.

C.1. **Inisheer**   (1988 - 1990) see ship No. M.24 in Arklow managed

C.2. **Inishowen** (1)   (1988 - 1990) see ship No. M.25 in Arklow managed

C.3. **Inishfree** (1)   (1988 - 1994) see ship No. M.21 in Arklow managed

C.4. **Inishark**   (1989 - 1997) see ship No. M.31 in Arklow managed

C.5. **Arklow Beach**   (1994 - 1995) see ship No. A.7 in Arklow owned.

C.6. **Arklow Valour**   (1995 -   ) see ship No. M.39 in Arklow managed

C.7. **Inishfree** (2)   (1996 - 2000) see ship No. M.58 in Arklow managed

C.8. **Inishowen** (2)   (1997 - 1998) see ship No. M.57 in Arklow managed

C.9. **Arklow Dawn** (2)   (1999 - 2003) see ship No. M.66 in Arklow managed

C.10. **Arklow Day** (2)   (2000 - 2003) see ship No. M.68 in Arklow managed

C.11. **Arklow Dusk**   (2000 - 2003) see ship No. M.69 in Arklow managed

C.12. **Arklow Wind**   (2003 -   ) see ship No. M.72 in Arklow managed

Hanno Shipping B. V.

(2002 : Restyled as Arklow Shipping Nederland B. V.)

7703015
Ned.1. **Bengalen** (1999 - 2002)
1,600g. 1,102n. 3,265d. 81,72m x 14,08m x 5,501m
Post 2002 : 1,951g. 1,047n. 3,265d.
12-cyl. 4 S.C.S.A. (220mm x 380mm) Brons 12TD200 Vee type engine by Brons Industrie Group, Alphen aan den Rijn.
2,400 bhp. 12.5 kts. Thwartship thrust propeller forward.

19.12.1977 : Keel laid as **Sylvia Omega** by Tille Scheepsbouw B. V., Kootstertille, (Yard No. 209), for Trias Cargo B.V., Rotterdam. 3.3.1978 : Launched for Sylvia Cargo B. V., Rotterdam. 15.4.1978 : Completed. 1985 : Sold to Rederij Combi Trader C.V., Rotterdam, (Heinrich Hanno & Company B. V., Rotterdam, managers), and renamed **Zomerhof**. 1993 : Sold to Bengalen Shipping Company N.V., Rotterdam, (Hanno - OAM Shipping V.o.f., Rotterdam, managers), Rotterdam, and renamed **Bengalen**. 1999 : Managers restyled as Hanno Shipping B.V. 11.2.2002 : Sold to Dolphin Shipping & Services S. A., Lattakia, Syria, and renamed **Anas J** under the Cambodia flag. 4.3.2002 : Seaboard Shipholding S.A. appointed managers. 4.4.2002 : Removed from management. 2004 : Still in *Lloyd's Register.*

Bengalen *on 2 February 1997 at Richardson's Wharf, Belfast.*

(Author's collection/Alan Geddes)

7703003
Ned.2. **Caspic** (1999 - 2002)
1,600g. 1,102n. 3,265d. 81,72m x 14,08m x 5,501m.
12-cyl. 4 S.C.S.A. (220mm x 380mm) Brons 12TD200 Vee type engine by Brons Industrie Group, Alphen aan den Rijn.
2,400 bhp. 12.5 kts. Thwartship thrust propeller forward.

19.9.1977 : Keel laid as **Sylvia Gamma** by Tille Scheepsbouw B. V., Kootstertille, (Yard No. 207) for Trias Cargo B.V., Rotterdam. 14.12.1977 : Launched for Sylvia Cargo B. V., Rotterdam. 27.1.1978 : Completed. 1985 : Sold to Rederij Combi Spirit C.V., Rotterdam, (Heinrich Hanno & Company B. V., Rotterdam, managers), and renamed **Vijverhof**. 1993 : Sold to Caspic Shipping Company N.V., Rotterdam, (Hanno - OAM Shipping V.o.f., Rotterdam, managers), and renamed **Caspic**. 1999 : Managers restyled as Hanno Shipping B.V. 2002 : Sold to Shady Shore Shipping, Lattakia, Syria, (Badri Shipping, Lattakia, Syria, managers), and renamed **Ghewa B** under the Cambodia flag. 2004 : Still in *Lloyd's Register.*

The crew on the **Caspic** are securing the first lines as the ship arrives at Llysfaen Jetty, Llanddulas, on 26 July 2000.

(D A Roberts)

8822612
Ned.3. **Cemile** (1999 - 2004)
O.N. 24185.   2,730g. 1,434n. 4,270d.   88,29m (BB) x 13,21m x 5,743m.
8-cyl. 4 S.C.S.A. (250mm x 300mm) Wärtsilä 8V25 Vee type engine by Wärtsilä Diesel Ab, Trollhättan, geared to a controllable pitch propeller. 2,298 bhp. 12 kts. Thwartship thrust propeller forward.

4.7.1990 : Keel laid by B. V. Scheepwerf "Ferus Smit", Foxhol, (Yard No. 265) for Carib Bird N. V., Rotterdam, (Sandfirden Rederij B. V., Rotterdam, managers), under the Netherlands Antilles flag. 23.3.1991 : Launched. 11.4.1991 : Completed. 1993 : Sold to Rederij Cemile B.V., Rotterdam, (Hanno- OAM Shipping V.o.f., Rotterdam, managers). 1999 : Managers restyled as Hanno Shipping B.V., managers. 2002 : Managers restyled as Arklow Shipping Nederland B.V. 29.6.2004 : Sold to Misje Rederi, Bergen, Norway; renamed **Cemi** under the Bahamas flag.

1996 was a Leap Year and it was on 29 February that the **Cemile** was photographed at the southern end of Graigola Wharf in Swansea's Kings Dock as she loaded coal for Ghent.

(Bill Moore)

7702918
Ned.4. **North Sea**   (1999 - 2002)
1,931g. 1,047n. 3,214d.   81,72m x 14,08m x 5,501m.
12-cyl. 4 S.C.S.A. (220mm x 380mm) Brons 12TD200 Vee type engine by Brons Industrie Group, Alphen aan den Rijn.
2,400 bhp. 12.5 kts. Thwartship thrust propeller forward.

16.5.1977 : Keel laid as **Sylvia Beta** by Appingedam Niestern Delfzijl B.V., Delfzijl, (Yard No. W. 496), for Trias Cargo B.V.,
Rotterdam.   30.11.1977 : Launched for Sylvia Cargo B. V., Rotterdam.   10.1.1978 : Completed.   1985 : Sold to
Kustvaartondernemming Elise B. V., Rotterdam, (Sandfirden B. V., Rotterdam, managers), and renamed **Elise**. 1992 :
Sold to Faerder Transport N.V., Rotterdam, (same managers), and renamed **North Sea**. 1993 : Hanno - OAM Shipping
V.o.f., Rotterdam, appointed as managers. 1999 : Managers restyled as Hanno Shipping B.V., managers. 11.2.2002 :
Sold to Dolphin Shipping & Services S. A., Lattakia, Syria, and renamed **Farouk J** under the Cambodia flag. 4.3.2002 :
Seaboard Shipholding S.A, appointed managers. 4.4.2002 : Removed from management. 2004 : Still in *Lloyd's Register*.

It was late in the evening of 2 June 1995 when the **North Sea** *was photographed as she passed the Hook of Holland on her way up
the New Waterway to Rotterdam.*

(Ian Willett)

8822600
Ned.5. **Magdalena**   (1999 -2004)
2,371g. 1,434n. 4,247d.   88,29m (BB) x 13,21m x 5,743m.
8-cyl. 4 S.C.S.A. (250mm x 300mm) Wärtsilä 8V25 Vee type engine by Wärtsilä Diesel Ab, Trollhättan, geared to a
controllable pitch propeller. 2,298 bhp. 12 kts. Thwartship thrust propeller forward.

23.3.1989 : Keel laid by B. V. Scheepwerf "Ferus Smit", Foxhol, (Yard No. 264) for Carib Sun N.V., Rotterdam, (Ocean-
Dolphin Ship Management (ODSM) N. V., managers), under Netherlands Antilles registry.   1993 : Sold to Rederij
Magdalena B.V., Rotterdam, (Hanno - OAM Shipping V.o.f., Rotterdam, managers). 19.6.1990 : Launched. 13.7.1990 :
Completed. 1999 : Managers restyled as Hanno Shipping B.V., managers. 2002 : Managers restyled as Arklow Shipping
Nederland B.V. 27.6.2004 : Sold to Ilze Shipping Co. Ltd., Riga, Latvia (Alpha Shipping Agency, Riga, managers);
transferred to Antigua & Barbuda flag.

9081356
Ned.6. **Ikiena**   (1999 -   )
O.N. 24491.   2,735g. 1,587n. 4,266d.   89,56m (BB) x 13,22m x 5,70m.
8-cyl. 4 S.C.S.A. (250mm x 300mm) Wärtsilä 8V25 Vee type engine by Wärtsilä Diesel Ab, Trollhättan, geared to a
controllable pitch propeller. 2,298 bhp. 12 kts. Thwartship thrust propeller forward.

General cargo vessel with a container capacity for 190 TEU.
6.5.1993 : Keel Laid by B. V. Scheepwerf "Ferus Smit", Foxhol, (Yard No. 294) for Rederij Ikiena B.V., Rotterdam, (Hanno
- OAM Shipping V.o.f., Rotterdam, managers). 10.9.1993 : Launched. 15.10.1993 : Completed. 1999 : Managers restyled
as Hanno Shipping B.V., managers. 2002 : Managers restyled as Arklow Shipping Nederland B.V.

The **Magdalena** loads a bulk cargo at Immingham on 19 March 2003. She departed for France the next day.

(Richard Potter)

The **Ikiena** is seen at Grimsby on 23 September 1997. The H O S on the funnel was later replaced by the Arklow badge once the Irish company took over Hanno - OAM Shipping. The Arklow badge is evident in the photograph on page 13.

(David H Smith)

9063873
Ned.7. **Marja** (1999 -   )
O.N. 25015.   2,715g. 1,586n. 4,293d.   89,80m (BB) x 13,19m x 5,54m.
As built : 8-cyl. 4 S.C.S.A. (250mm x 300mm) Wärtsilä 8V25 Vee type engine by Wärtsilä Diesel Ab, Trollhättan, geared
to a controllable pitch propeller. 2,298 bhp. 12 kts. Thwartship thrust propeller forward.
Post 1995 : 6-cyl. 4 S.C.S.A. (280mm x 300mm) Stork - Wärtsilä 6SW280 type engine by Stork - Wärtsilä Diesel B.V.,
Zwolle. 2,298 bhp

General cargo vessel with a 197 TEU container capacity. 117 hold/80 deck.
24.8.1992 : Keel laid by Scheepswerf Bijholt B.V., Foxhol, (Yard No. 689), for Rederij Combi Spirit C. V. Rotterdam,
(Heinrich Hanno & Company B. V., Rotterdam, managers). 16.7.1993 : Launched. 15.10.1993 : Completed. 1993 :
Transferred to Rederij Marja B.V., Rotterdam, (Hanno - OAM Shipping V.o.f., Rotterdam, managers). 8.1995 : Re-engined.
1999 : Managers restyled as Hanno Shipping B.V., managers. 2002 : Managers restyled as Arklow Shipping Nederland
B.V.

The **Marja** loads wheat for Belfast at Boston on 18 March 2003. The funnel of this ship bears the Arklow badge.

(David Dixon)

9081344
Ned.8. **Katja** (1999 -   )
O.N. 24898.   2,753g. 1,587n. 4,250d.   89,56m(BB) x 13,22m x 5,70m.
8-cyl. 4 S.C.S.A. (250mm x 300mm) Wärtsilä 8V25 Vee type engine by Wärtsilä Diesel Ab, Trollhättan, geared to a
controllable pitch propeller. 2,298 bhp. 12 kts. Thwartship thrust propeller forward.

11.2.1993 : Keel laid by B. V. Scheepwerf "Ferus Smit", Foxhol, (Yard No. 293) for Rederij Katja B.V., Rotterdam, (Hanno
- OAM Shipping V.o.f., Rotterdam, managers). 13.6.1993 : Launched. 2.8.1993 : Completed. 1999 : Managers restyled
as Hanno Shipping B.V., managers. 2002 : Managers restyled as Arklow Shipping Nederland B.V.

9063885
Ned.9. **Marjolein** (1999 -   )
O.N. 25312.   2,715g. 1,586n. 4,293d.   89,80m (BB) x 13,19m x 5,54m.
As built : 8-cyl. 4 S.C.S.A. (250mm x 300mm) Wärtsilä 8V25 Vee type engine by Wärtsilä Diesel Ab, Trollhättan, geared
to a controllable pitch propeller. 2,298 bhp. 12 kts. Thwartship thrust propeller forward.

General cargo vessel with a 197 TEU container capacity. 117 hold/80 deck.
9.11.1992 : Keel laid by Scheepswerf Bijholt B.V., Foxhol, (Yard No. 690), for Rederij Marjolein B.V., Rotterdam, (Hanno -
OAM Shipping V.o.f., Rotterdam, managers). 9.4.1994 : Launched. 19.5.1994 : Completed. 1999 : Managers restyled
as Hanno Shipping B.V., managers. 2002 : Managers restyled as Arklow Shipping Nederland B.V.

The **Katja** loads steel scrap at Berth 2 in Chatham Docks on 28 March 2001. This was the second such cargo loaded for scrap dealers Easimet.

(Peter Hutchison)

Marjolein was photographed as she headed along the New Waterway on 26 April 1995.

(Jan van der Klooster)

7702994
Ned.10. **Scotia**   (1999 - 2002)
1,951g. 1,047n. 3,214d.   81,72m x 14,10m x 5,501m.
12-cyl. 4 S.C.S.A. (220mm x 380mm) Brons 12TD200 Vee type engine by Brons Industrie Group, Alphen aan den Rijn.
2,400 bhp. 12.5 kts. Thwartship thrust propeller forward.

15.4.1977 : Keel laid as **Sylvia Alpha** by Tille Scheepsbouw B. V., Kootstertille, (Yard No. 206), for Trias Cargo B. V.,
Rotterdam. 16.9.1977 : Launched for Sylvia Cargo B.V., Rotterdam. 1.11.1977 : Completed. 1985 : Sold to Rederij Linde
Lloyd VII, Rotterdam, (Sandfirden B.V., Rotterdam, managers), and renamed **Reestland**. 1987 : Sold to Carib Bird N.V.,
Rotterdam, (Otto A. Muller GmbH, Hamburg, managers), and renamed **Carib Bird** under Netherlands Antilles registry.
1988 : Sold to Kustvaartondernemming Elise B. V., Rotterdam, (Sandfirden B. V., Rotterdam, managers), and renamed
Katja. 1991 : Sold to Rederij Vredehof B.V., Rotterdam, (Heinrich Hanno & Company B.V., Rotterdam, managers), and
renamed **Vredehof**. 1993 : Sold to Scotia Shipping Company N.V. Rotterdam, (Hanno-OAM Shipping V.o.f., Rotterdam,
managers), and renamed **Scotia**. 1999 : Managers restyled as Hanno Shipping B.V., managers. 2002 : Sold to Prime
Marine & Trading S. A., Beirut, Lebanon, (Abourjeily Ship Management, Beirut, managers), and renamed **Brothers Start**
under the Cambodia flag. 2004 : Still in *Lloyd's Register*.

With the "new" Severn
Bridge in the background,
the **Scotia** approaches
Avonmouth on 2 June 2001
at the end of a voyage from
Antwerp. She departed for
Amsterdam two days later.

(John Southwood)

7359137
Ned.11. **Combi Trader**   (1999 - 2000)
1,399g. 867n. 2,807d.   71,48m x 13,03m x 5,735m.
Post 1999 :   1,618g. 971n. 2,807d.
6-cyl. 4 S.C.S.A. (320mm x 420mm), MaK 6M453AK type oil engine by MaK Maschinenbau GmbH, Kiel. 2,000 bhp. 13
kts.

General cargo vessel with a 64 TEU container capacity.
14.1.1975 : Keel laid by Ørskovs Staalskibsværft I/S., Frederikshavn, (Yard No. 74), for KS Bewa, Denmark. 4.3.1975 :
Launched as **Ocean Coast** for Hans J. Therkildsen, Næstved, Denmark. 30.5.1975 : Completed. 1975 : Sold to Rederij
Combi Trader B.V., Rotterdam, (Heinrich Hanno & Company B.V., Rotterdam, managers), and renamed **Combi Trader**.
1993 : Managers restyled as Hanno - OAM Shipping V.o.f. 1999 : Managers restyled as Hanno Shipping B.V., managers.
12.5.2000 : Sold to World Shipping Charters S. A., Miami, (World Shipping Management Corp., Miami, managers), under
the Panama flag. 2004 : Still in *Lloyd's Register*.

9196266
Ned.12. **Arklow Sky**   (2000 -   )
2,316g. 1,295n. 3,193d.   89,98m x 12,64m x 4,652m.
8-cyl. 4 S.C.S.A. (200mm x 300mm) MaK 8M20 type oil engine by MaK Motoren GmbH & Co KG, Kiel, single reduction
reverse geared to screw shaft with fixed pitch propeller. 2,066 bhp. 12.5 kts. Thwartship thrust propeller forward.

General cargo vessel strengthened for heavy cargoes and with a 154 TEU container capacity. 114 hold/40 deck.
30.6.1998 : Keel laid by Schps. & Mfbk. Barkmeijer Stroobos B. V., Stroobos, (Yard No. 291), for Arklow Shipping B. V.,
Netherlands. 31.3.2000 : Launched. 26.4.2000 : Completed for Scheepvaartmij Titania B. V., Rotterdam, (Hanno Shipping
B.V., Rotterdam, managers). 2002 : Managers restyled as Arklow Shipping Nederland B.V. 2004 : Still in *Lloyd's Register*.

9250414
Ned.13. **Arklow Rally** (2002 -   )
2,999g. 1,671n. 4,400d.   89,95m x 14,40m x 5,79m.
6-cyl. 4 S.C.S.A. (255mm x 400mm) MaK 6M25 type oil engine by Caterpillar Motoren GmbH & Co KG, Kiel, single reduction reverse geared to screw shaft with controllable pitch propeller. 2,447 bhp. 11 kts. Thwartship thrust propeller forward.

27.12.2000 : Keel laid by Scheepswerf Biljsma Lemmer B. V., Lemmer, (Yard No. 699), for Arklow Shipping Ltd. 2.3.2002 : Launched. 26.4.2002 : Completed for C.V. Scheepvaartonderneming Arklow 1, Rotterdam, (Arklow Shipping Nederland B. V., Rotterdam, managers).

*Photographed at St Malo on 19 May 2002, the **Arklow Rally** had been in service for less than a month. She had just arrived from Casablanca and departed for Rouen three days later.*

(Peter Stewart)

*Waiting for a berth at Tilbury Grain Terminal, the **Arklow Rambler** rests at Tilbury Landing Stage on 28 August 2002. She had brought her cargo of grain from Bordeaux. She left for Rotterdam two days later.*

(Kevin Bassett)

9250426
Ned.14. **Arklow Rambler** (2002 -   )
2,999g. 1,671n. 4,400d.   89,95m x 14,40m x 5,79m.
6-cyl. 4 S.C.S.A. (255mm x 400mm) MaK 6M25 type oil engine by Caterpillar Motoren GmbH & Co KG, Kiel, single reduction reverse geared to screw shaft with controllable pitch propeller. 2,447 bhp. 11 kts. Thwartship thrust propeller forward.

27.12.2000 : Keel laid by Scheepswerf Biljsma Lemmer B. V., Lemmer, (Yard No. 700), for Arklow Shipping Ltd. 23.5.2002 : Launched. 27.6.2002 : Completed for C.V. Scheepvaartonderneming Arklow 2, Rotterdam, (Arklow Shipping Nederland B.V., Rotterdam, managers).

The **Arklow Rambler** at Lemmer on 2 June 2002. She had been launched only ten days previously.

(Dominic McCall)

*Having arrived from Tilbury the previous day, the **Arklow Ranger** loads grain in Grimsby's Royal Dock on 7 August 2003. She sailed two days later to Corunna.*

(Jordan Seifarth)

9250438
Ned.15. **Arklow Ranger**   (2002 -   )
2,999g. 1,671n. 4,400d.   89,95m x 14,40m x 5,79m.
6-cyl. 4 S.C.S.A. (255mm x 400mm) MaK 6M25 type oil engine by Caterpillar Motoren GmbH & Co KG, Kiel, single reduction reverse geared to screw shaft with controllable pitch propeller. 2,447 bhp. 11 kts. Thwartship thrust propeller forward.

27.12.2000 : Keel laid by Scheepswerf Biljsma Lemmer B. V., Lemmer, (Yard No. 701), for Arklow Shipping Ltd. 2.8.2002 : Launched. 9.9.2002 : Completed for C.V. Scheepvaartonderneming Arklow 3, Rotterdam, (Arklow Shipping Nederland B.V., Rotterdam, managers).

Ned.16. **Arklow Sand**   (2002 -   ) see ship No. M.63 above.

Ned.17. **Arklow Sea**   (2002 -   ) see ship No. M.64 above.

Ned.18. **Arklow Star**   (2002 -   ) see ship No. M.65 above.

The **Arklow Star** arrives at Sutton Bridge from Immingham on 27 August 2000. She was about to load a cargo of wheat for delivery to Belfast.

(John Lucas)

Bibliography

Carebeka 1939 – 1983 by J. H. Andereisse, E. A. Kruidhof & J. Oostmeijer (World Ship Society, 1995)
Mersey Rovers by R. S. Fenton (World Ship Society, 1997)
Cambrian Coasters by R. S. Fenton (World Ship Society, 1989)
Maritime Arklow by Frank Forde (Glendale Press Ltd., 1988)
Around the Coast and Across the Seas by Nigel Watson (St. Matthew's Press, 2000)
Lloyd's Register of Shipping for all relevant years.
Lloyd's Confidential Index for all relevant years.
Lloyd's Casualty Returns.
Lloyd's Register of International Shipping Groups.
Marine News – Monthly journal of the World Ship Society.

In Later Guise

The distinctive green hulls of the present Arklow fleet make for instant recognition in port or at sea. Some vessels sold out of the fleet have kept the same colours although rarely maintained in as good condition. Others have been repainted. The **Arklow River** (1) traded successfully for Isle of Man owners Mezeron Ltd between 1988 and 1997. On 16 February 1991, she approaches Glasson Dock to load more general cargo for the Isle of Man. Following her sale to a Canadian owner in early 1997, it was reported that she had been re-engined and equipped with two deck cranes. Her new trade took her to Greenland, Baffin Island and Goose Bay.

(Bernard McCall)

The **River Avoca** (2) has had an uncertain career since her sale in 1997. She has been laid up in Poole and Portland, but it was whilst she was laid up at Oreston Quay in Plymouth that she was photographed on 8 April 2002. She had been renamed **Torch** when converted and used as a buoy tender on the River Clyde.

(Bernard McCall)

Arklow Dawn photo feature

*This photograph must have been taken shortly after the **Arklow Dawn** had come into Arklow ownership. The letter G on the funnel was the mark of her previous owners, Golden Fair Shipping S.A., and her hull bore the letters R S L to denote her charterers. The letter R was conveniently changed to A, thus making the initial letters of Arklow Shipping Ltd.*

(Author's collection)

Now without deck cranes, the ship discharges animal feed at Royal Portbury Dock on 24 September 2003.

(Dominic McCall)

On the same occasion as the previous photograph, we now look out over the deck from the bridge wing with the bases of the cranes and associated equipment clearly visible.

(Dominic McCall)

In the wheelhouse with radars and control panels in view.

(Dominic McCall)

Index

Bold italic names refer to those ships that had Group involvement.
Other names are those of the ships prior to or following Group involvement.
The numbers on the right of the name refer to the relevant page(s) in the book.

92

Addendum : We are grateful to Mr James Tyrrell for pointing out that the **Alfred Mason** (page 17) was not owned by any of the Arklow Shipping Ltd companies or personnel. Mr Tyrrell believes that she was owned by John Tyrrell, Ferrybank, Arklow, who may have used John Tyrrell Ltd, Cardiff, as his agent in buying her.

When compiling a book about a modern proactive shipping company whose fleet is being constantly updated to meet new trading opportunities, it is difficult to ensure that all details are up-to-date when the book goes to press. All fleet lists are correct up to July 2004, and some additions have been made since then. On the very day that the book goes to the printers, we have received news that the company has just acquired another vessel, the **Swan** *(NLD, 2839gt/95) which has been renamed* **Arklow Swan**. *Our photograph shows her at Dordrecht on 18 October 2004, soon after being handed over and renamed at Schiedam.*

(Reinier van de Wetering, courtesy Riversea International)

Back cover : We hope that this book has given readers a thorough insight into this fascinating company, indeed an **Arklow View**! *The ship is seen on the Manchester Ship Canal in September 1996.*

(Stan Tedford)